TALES OF BAPTIST DARING

Tales of Baptist Daring

by Benjamin P. Browne

Illustrations by William Hamilton

THE JUDSON PRESS
Philadelphia • Chicago • Los Angeles

Printed in the U.S.A.

CONTENTS

INTRODUCTION

THE DAY SEEMS OVERDUE for the present generation of Baptists to become better acquainted with their Baptist forefathers. This can be done without any apology, for the men who gave them their heritage were men of faith, insight, and courage — men of whom they may justly feel proud. Indeed, some of them rank among the noblest characters in all of history.

Surely, the adults of every good family will want to pass on to the younger generation the best of its heritage. Furthermore, since the past inevitably lives on in the present, it will be impossible to understand our faith today apart from a knowledge of those who made its heroic yesterdays. The soil in which any seed grows conditions its fruit, and the roots of a plant are vital to its flowering. Blossoms do not long endure when cut off from the root and stock.

Neither is there anything narrow or bigoted in becoming informed about those on whose shoulders we stand. Indeed, there would be something ignoble in us if we were willing to forget those rugged pioneers who blazed the trail through the thickets where we now may walk without fear of the whiplash of a branch across our face, the cut of a stone upon our foot, or even a scratch upon our skin. For example, to remember William Carey, the impoverished cobbler-scholar, or Adoniram Judson, the tortured prisoner of a pockmarked Burmese jailer, is but to challenge ourselves to more vigorous efforts, to larger tasks, and to more dedicated discipleship.

Our Baptist forefathers were personalities who belonged to the kingdom of God in its wider aspects, for their prophetic insights and convincing voices added new depths and dimensions to man's understanding of the meaning and fullness of God's kingdom. Thomas Helwys was the first in England to proclaim liberty of thought and expression in matters of conscience toward God. John Bunyan was the first to create a popular Christian book which still stands in "the best-seller class," and thus introduced a fresh medium for communicating the gospel. William Carey was the first to stir up the sleeping Protestant world to the challenge of the missionary enterprise, and he is everywhere rightly recognized as "the Father of the Modern Missionary Movement." Adoniram Judson, by carrying the gospel to Burma, was the first to arouse Americans in a big way to the challenge of missions. Charles Haddon Spurgeon was the first evangelical preacher to have his sermons printed and avidly read by millions on two continents. Walter Rauschenbusch was the first to awaken the modern conscience to the social demands of the gospel and to give those demands scholarly status. But why go on? A whole chapter could be written about the frontiers where Baptists have been "firsts" and pioneers. In any event, our Baptist forebears by their courageous convictions and adventurous daring have enriched the life and thought of all Christendom.

It is the sincere desire of the writer that these chapters, in which the lives of the heroes who went before us are recalled, may serve to brighten the flame of our present-day faith, which too often gives forth only a feeble flicker. By the reading of this book in family groups as one of the projects of the Baptist Jubilee Advance, it is hoped that a new dynamic of faith may grip our family life and, in turn, the life of all our churches. As we come to know our Baptist inheritance we should become all the stronger as Christians.

While the author has made every effort to keep the book historically oriented and accurate as to dates and facts, he has highlighted conversations and scenes with a degree of historical imagination.

The writer extends special thanks to Ethelyn Parkinson for her suggested revisions of some chapters, to Norman H. Maring and Norman A. Baxter for their reading of the manuscript to check historical backgrounds, to Margaret

Ward for her technical assistance, and to Miles W. Smith and Ellwood S. Wolf for their consummate skill as editors.

To the worthy purpose of the Baptist Jubilee Advance, the pages of this book are prayerfully committed.

BENJAMIN P. BROWNE

Philadelphia, Pa.

January 15, 1961

CHAPTER 1

ROGER WILLIAMS

A Pioneer of Liberty

IN THE LOG-CABIN COURTHOUSE in Boston one wintry day, a company of black-robed Puritan magistrates sat in solemn judgment upon a most vexing and troublesome — though absent — man.

"Hanging is too good for him!" The First Magistrate of the General Court brought his fist down upon the table with a thunderous bang. "This Roger Williams must be silenced, even if we have to take him a hundred miles out into the Atlantic Ocean and set him adrift in a canoe!"

The colleague seated next to him was less harsh and more prudent. "Don't forget," he warned, "that Elder Williams was ordained by the Church of England as a godly minister when he was but thirty-two years old."

"Well, he is no 'godly minister' to us," a third and bilious-faced dignitary responded dourly.

"But remember," Williams' defender admonished, "in England none other than the powerful Sir Edward Coke was once his friend. So, too, was Sir William Masham. This Williams is a man of parts. Besides, he is not simple. He is a graduate of Pembroke College, Cambridge, — a scholar who speaks six languages."

"Aye, a pity!" the First Magistrate observed. "For he makes too much trouble by speaking in one." He waited for the point to sink in, then glowered: "If I had a pair of pincers, I'd like to yank out that tongue of his. His ranting about 'religious freedom' and 'holding aloft the torch of

11

liberty' will be the undoing of our colony, if we don't put a stop to him, and that right shortly!"

Through loose-fitting windows, the cold east wind from Boston harbor blew into the courtroom. A lean-faced magistrate stirred, drew in a deep and reassuring breath of the salt ocean air that came straight from off the clam flats, and loudly spoke his mind.

"This Roger Williams is a pest and a plague. With his heretical beliefs, he is unsettling our colony. The Scriptures warn us to have no dealings with such a man. We must have him arrested forthwith. If we are not ready to hang a minister, then by all that is holy, let us banish him far hence, to England. Get him out of our colony, I say." Waving his hands as he grew more excited, he stood, shouting: "I will have no more of this windbag, with his false teaching about freedom and about paying the Indians a larger price for the land. I say, away with him!"

Satisfied that the court was behind him, and now all smiles for having won his point, the First Magistrate spoke:

"We had best do our intention under the protection of darkness, while Williams and his friends can be caught asleep. This queer independent did not yield to our earlier demand that he accept banishment from the colony. Instead, he pleaded delay because of his ill health. We did therefore grant him our temporary mercy, but now I believe it to be our wisest course to banish him to England. If he be gone from the land before it be known, no one can have complaint of us. And by God's grace I have a plan, if you leave it to me."

"We do, we do, indeed." The judges nodded piously, and stroked their beards. Then, pulling their cloaks about them, all but the First Magistrate stepped out into the biting air.

For a moment the First Magistrate sat alone, reflecting upon this man, Roger Williams, and the danger he had brought to the peace and security of the colony.

The Boston of 1635 was only a little log-cabin settlement planted on three hills as a clearing in a dark, surrounding forest where Indians skulked.

12   In the very center of the town were a cow pasture and a

pond where a chorus of frogs croaked in diapason all night. There were no carts or automobiles, and no streets as we know them today. People walked along muddy paths which were made by the trampling cows.

Toward the east, the Puritan settlers could look out on the glittering Atlantic Ocean and the beautiful harbor strewn with evergreen islands. Ten miles to the north through the woods was another cabin settlement called Salem, where a few years later the Puritans would hang "witches" on Gallows Hill. Thirty miles to the south was Plymouth, where the Pilgrims first landed in 1620, and where John Alden and Priscilla Mullens fell in love.

All the men and women who had settled in Boston were of the stiffest and sternest sort. They had turned their backs on their homeland for the sake of their religious beliefs.

Braving a long and perilous ocean voyage in little unseaworthy ships, they had come, as pioneers, to an untamed wilderness. There they had founded a colony with rules to be strictly obeyed by every person within it.

The Puritan men were as severe as they looked, with their broad-brimmed, tall black hats above bearded faces, their plain-cut dark cloaks, knee breeches, and buckled shoes.

They had paid a big price in separation, sacrifice, and hardship to get the Massachusetts Bay Colony started. Therefore they were not willing to put up with anyone who would not agree with their doctrines and laws for governing it. Their leaders did not intend to permit any interference, not even from so well-educated a minister as Roger Williams of Salem!

Williams had become unpopular with the officers of the colony when he began to preach independent beliefs. Soon the Puritan leaders began to fear his new ideas about the difference between civil and religious obedience. He was saying too much about the freedom of each man's conscience before God.

"Too much!" Alone in the courtroom, the Chief Magistrate spoke aloud. "He must be stopped."

He glanced out the window to where a two-masted sailing vessel lay at anchor in the harbor.

"Wainwright!" he whispered.

He arose and strode purposefully through the door.

Outside the building, his burly hulk sprawled across a wooden bench, a red-faced sea captain sat awaiting orders.

He pulled himself to his feet in respect, as the First Magistrate addressed him: "Captain Wainwright, we want you to sail your ship out of Boston Harbor late this afternoon. Slip you to anchorage silently in Salem Harbor, just about dark. You, Captain, and two members of your crew, go to the log house of Elder Roger Williams, the ranting independent. Place him under arrest by order of this General Court. Here are the papers.

"I hope you catch him in bed. Before the town is awakened, hustle him in chains to your ship and be off to England before dawn breaks. In brief, your orders are: 'Go fetch the heretic, Roger Williams, and remove him far hence, for the sake of peace in our colony, and God be with you. You will be doing His will.'"

"Aye, sir." The captain saluted, and tightened his double-breasted coat with its brass buttons. "I am the man to carry out your orders. I have battled with pirates, so why should a separatist and heretic be more to me than a poor fish stranded on the shore?" He roared a sinister guffaw, rubbing his rough hands together.

"The scoundrel's escaped!" cried the angered captain to his crew that night. They had searched the house in Salem, and had found no trace of Williams. They had pounded upon door after door, demanding of startled and sleepy householders: "Can you tell us aught of the whereabouts of Elder Roger Williams?"

Strange to say, the good people of Salem somehow could not seem to recall having seen Williams lately, nor, when pressed for answers, could they even by the most vigorous scratching of their heads produce a suggestion of where he might have gone.

Though Roger Williams escaped the trap set for him that time, still the order of banishment hung over his head, and he knew only too well that before long his enemies would catch up with him.

14

No persecution is more relentless than religious persecution. Although he had successfully dodged the first order of banishment given on October 19, 1635, he knew that time was running out. He must flee quickly into exile in order to escape something worse, — either his forced return to England without his family or even his death.

There was no place of refuge except the wilderness, with its Indians. To the wilderness he turned, frail of health and alone, but strong in his purposes.

The northeast wind drove the stinging hail, like a thousand knife-points, into Elder Williams' face. He lowered his head, pulled his broad-brimmed hat low over his brow, and tightened his black cloth cloak around his shivering body, as he trudged through the deep snow of his forest exile.

It was January of 1636. In New England the days were short. Dark came early. It was a bitter winter and the snow was very deep. Williams felt alone.

A deer nibbling at the bark of a tree gazed in friendly wonderment.

Williams had traveled but six miles that first day. Now, darkness was falling. He must stop to build a bed of fir branches in some sheltered place, for he would need to rest.

As he worked, he heard someone behind him. He turned quickly and looked upon a well-known and welcome face. A faithful servant of his household had followed him, determined to share his hardships and ease his loneliness.

Williams was grateful. With a little fire of sticks and water from under the ice in a stream, he made herb tea to warm them from the chill that cut to the marrow of their bones. He had traveled light. His pack contained little beyond a sun dial to help him tell the time, his Bible to feed his soul, and a loaf of bread to feed his body.

As they broke the bread together, he told his servant: "Some things I have brought with me that are not in my pack. I have brought along a stout heart to endure persecution because of what I know to be God's truth. I praise God that I may suffer for Christ's sake and for the cause of liberty of conscience for all men."

In the morning, his limbs stiff from his hard bed and the   15 cold, Williams plunged bravely on. He knew that, although he must live out the winter in the wilderness, he had some friends among the native Indians. The "Christian" Puritans had banished him, but some of the "heathen" Indians would welcome him. Fortunately he escaped the hostile Pequots, because they were snowbound. He passed beyond their borders and approached the friendly Narragansetts. He had always traded fairly with them, never cheating them. Now he could hope for their help, when he so greatly needed it.

Some friendly Narragansett Indians found him when by the third day he had penetrated the forest about thirty miles. For a time he made that place his shelter against the storms and cold.

Good cheer came to his forest hideout when four brave-hearted members of his Salem church came to join him in his exile. With them were his wife, Mary, and his two children — one only a few months old.

In June of that exile year, Williams with these companions pushed a canoe across the river. They pressed on, to discover a cool spring of fresh water. Standing there upon a rock, he named the place Providence and gave thanks to God. Thus was founded a great city of the future.

Perhaps Williams had other reasons for calling this new colony Providence. Perhaps he remembered his first serious love affairs and how strangely providence had turned a bitter experience to his good.

In his youth, back in England, he had fallen deeply in love with Jane, a dainty and beautiful girl whose guardian was an aristocratic aunt, Lady Barrington. When Williams, a poor young minister without property or visible prospects, made bold to ask the hand of her lovely niece, this lady, in great indignation, had him banished from the girl's presence. Williams was never to see her again.

He had loved and lost. It was as well. That delicate first love, reared in the grand manner, could never have endured the rigors of primitive frontier life in the new world of Plymouth and Salem. Much less would her upbringing have enabled her to accept the experiences and hardships of wintry exile in forests and among Indians.

16

In despair over his rejection, and in a kind of emotional rebound, Roger Williams had married a maid in the household, a girl named Mary Barnard, who had been an attendant of Lady Barrington.

The physically strong, hard-muscled, and capable Mary was just the wife to stand shoulder to shoulder with her man in exile, to bear his children, and to rear them in hardship.

Too, she was devout, a wife who prayed with him.

Without the encouragement and loyalty of Mary, whom he deeply loved, he might have faltered. He might not have been so brave.

It is not hard to believe that God's goodness in guiding his choice of a wife may have entered his mind and heart when he named the spot Providence. Slowly, as others joined it, the colony grew. Soon the leaders drew up a compact governing themselves "only in civil things."

Four years later, in 1640, they introduced a great new idea to the new world. They agreed that liberty of conscience was to be the ruling principle of the Providence Plantations.

Thus they declared: "We agree as formerly both in the liberties of this town, so still to hold forth liberty of conscience."

Though Roger Williams, for the sake of independent belief, was driven from his English homeland as a youth ("Truly," he wrote, "it was bitter as death when Bishop Lane pursued me out of the land"), and ultimately was driven to the founding of a new colony, he thereby provided a homeland of freedom for all exiles and refugees from tyranny.

Roger Williams was but thirty-five years of age when he gave the world this new pattern of freedom and liberty of conscience.

As the years have rolled on, the city of Providence has not forgotten its founder. A beautiful park of many acres which adorns the city is known as Roger Williams Park. Here, too, one may see the rock on which Williams first landed. His benign but spiritually strong figure stands immortalized in sculpture overlooking the city which he made a haven for lovers of freedom. The tall-spired First Baptist Church of

Providence, in white colonial architecture, is the church he organized in 1639, having first been baptized himself.

Right gladly today do Baptists salute Roger Williams as more than a fellow believer. They salute him as the man who first climbed the towering heights to plant the flag of freedom — religious and civil — victorious over America.

Friend of Cromwell, Milton, John Clarke, the Indians, and every refugee seeking asylum, his name will shine with undimmed lustre so long as men love liberty above life.

Before his earthly mission as a "seeker" ended, Roger Williams took the long sea voyage back to England, the home he had left as a young man, so many years before.

But he returned to the mother country only in the interest of his new colony of Providence. Above all things, he desired a secure charter which would guarantee and preserve this big new idea in the new world — liberty in matters of conscience for all men of every race, creed, and color.

After weary months he sailed again for the new world with the royal charter safe in his hands. It was the triumphant fulfillment of a long dream, the reward of his undaunted labor and pioneer daring.

The voyage to Boston was safely made. The news of the ship's arrival there reached Providence, and his rejoicing wife and friends prepared a welcome for him. The Indians smeared their bodies with red, blue, and yellow paint. The chiefs donned their brilliant cascades of feathers. When Williams waved from the other shore of the river, the colorful company clambered into fourteen canoes made of white and yellow birch bark and set forth to meet him.

The setting sun threw a soft red glow across the rippling water. The measured strokes of the paddles, held in the strong brown hands, bore the fleet of shining canoes swiftly forward.

As they touched shore the Indians, beating their hands across their open mouths, gave a loud call of greeting and welcome.

"Wa-Wa-Wa . . .!"

Williams responded from a heart almost too full for speech.

18

The Indians ran forward and lifted him to their shoulders. Moments later, they put him down beside Mary, his wife.

He put his arms around her and held her close, and kissed her; then held her back, and smiled into her eyes.

"Mary," he murmured. "Mary. This *is* Providence, and no mistake!"

Roger Williams

CHAPTER 2

JOHN CLARKE and OBADIAH HOLMES

Whipped with Roses

"STAND FORTH, Anne Hutchinson," thundered Elder John Wilson from the high pulpit of the First Church of the Puritans in Boston on a March Sunday in 1638. "You woman of dangerous errors, you servant of Satan, I denounce you in the house of God."

Now, Anne Hutchinson, the daughter of an English rector of London, was a very bright and independently minded woman who had turned nonconformist. For some time she had been sending shivers of fear and jealousy up and down the spines of the stiff-necked Puritan preachers of Boston; and for one simple reason: with her interest and skill in theological discussion, she had gathered more people every Thursday afternoon at her house on Washington Street to hear her talk about theology than went on Sunday to the meeting house to hear the elders preach. In a woman, this was unforgivable; and besides, she had defied the opinions of the preachers to their face. They, accordingly, had accused her of holding eighty-two "erroneous opinions." Anne now stood in solemn silence before the hushed congregation. "I do cast you out as a leper that you no more blaspheme, seduce, and lie," shouted the elder. "I do hereby deliver you over to Satan. I do order the congregation to treat you as a heathen and a publican."

Thus, the heavy blow of excommunication and banishment fell on this persecuted woman. The Puritan General Court was bent on striking fear into the heart of anyone who might dare to defy it or to hold different religious doctrines.

As Anne, the mother of fourteen children, slowly walked down the aisle of the meeting house, hate-filled eyes blazed around her. She searched the congregation for one look of pity upon her plight. Suddenly, little Mary Dyer leaped to her feet, came to her side, and took her arm. Together they walked out of the church into the raw east wind blowing in from Boston harbor. At sight of this act of kindness, the elders gnashed their teeth and the congregation hissed. Knowingly they nodded their heads. "Mary Dyer will pay for this," they whispered, for the stern Puritans held it a crime to give any comfort to a heretic.

Twenty-four years later, Mary Dyer, who had become a Quakeress, felt the full force of the Puritan vengeance in a never-to-be-forgotten martyrdom. That day, the cows grazing in the pasture land of Boston Common looked up with bovine curiosity at the unusually large crowd gathering there. The boys who were sailing their homemade boats on the frog pond came running to see what the excitement was about. They saw a crude scaffold being erected and Mary Dyer, the Quakeress, standing in chains. To their horror they saw her dragged weeping to the platform. A rope noose was put around her throat; a black hood was dropped over her head. Then, to the screams of the hysterical women in the crowd, they saw the body of Mary Dyer lurch, jerk, and dangle by the neck in the last convulsion of death. The crowd dispersed slowly. "She was a vile Quakeress," they said. "Yea, she held pernicious and dangerous doctrines," others added.

The groundwork for such revolting outbreaks of bigotry and persecution as these was laid in the Massachusetts Bay Colony in the early days. Severe persecution befell a number of men of independent spirit, among them the six-foot tall, magnetic John Clarke, the physician, and the sinewy-muscled Obadiah Holmes, the glassmaker. Both of them, when young men, had come to America in order to get away from the persecution for religious beliefs taking place in England. Yet they found much the same situation in Massachusetts.

The twenty-nine-year-old Clarke wrote: "A year in this hotbed of religious tyranny is enough for me. I cannot bear to see men in these uttermost parts of the earth not able to bear with others in matters of conscience and live peaceably together. With so much land before us, I for one will turn aside, shake the dust of Boston off my feet, and betake me to a new place. There I shall make a haven for all those who, like myself, are disgusted and sickened by the Puritan dictatorship. I shall make it a place where there will be full freedom of thought and religious conscience."

This decision to go to a new wilderness frontier was not easy to make. Deep in thought, he rested his head in his two hands. "I can support myself wherever I go, for I practiced medicine in London. With my training at the University of Leyden in Holland, I certainly can keep up with any stray doctors here in this wilderness," he smiled to himself.

He stood up suddenly, and doubling his right fist he brought it down hard into his open left hand. "The more I see of this religious tyranny over men's minds and the more I read my New Testament, the more I am convinced that the Baptists I associated with in Holland have the right of it. Religious liberty is the birthright of every man. The state has no right whatever to dictate to a man's conscience before God. I am for a free church in a free state."

With that, Clarke started packing. Remembering the experience of Roger Williams, he decided not to wait for the General Court to banish him officially. He already was under suspicion for his independent beliefs.

While some of his friends went by ship, Clarke trekked to Providence, R.I., to get the advice of Williams regarding a settlement in a new location. Clarke and his friends chose the island spot now called Newport, R.I. There, in 1644, he organized a Baptist church. Meanwhile he kept open house for other refugees from Puritan persecution. Lovers of liberty joined his colony in numbers, and many of the leading citizens and choicest spirits of Boston left that city and joined him in order that they too might enjoy the fruits of freedom of conscience.

Of those who came to Newport, none was more courageous than Obadiah Holmes, the glassmaker of Salem, Mass. He was a graduate of Oxford University and a man of parts. And thereby hangs a tale, for Clarke and Holmes became fast friends, and together they gave a still glittering demonstration of Baptist principles and of bravery in defending them.

Obadiah Holmes had sailed from England when he was about thirty years of age, and he had set up in Salem in 1639 what is said to have been the first glassworks in the United States. His business partner, Lawrence Southwick, was an Independent. Soon enough, as you may imagine, Holmes and Southwick, being independent thinkers, were in trouble with the meddling Puritans. The General Court was quick to sniff the first whiff of what they considered heresy.

So the General Court moved in on poor Southwick, and levied heavy fines upon him just for being an Independent. Southwick did not have the money with which to pay these fines. So what did the monstrous General Court do but order Southwick's children, a girl and a boy, to be sold into slavery! How the devilish plan failed, can now be told, if we may use a bit of imagination in recreating the scene.

One morning while her husband was at work, Mother Southwick's home was entered by constables who seized her two children. "Where are you taking my children, and why?" she screamed in terror. "By order of the General Court, they are to be sold into slavery in some foreign country," the constables answered in cold-blooded voices. "The money from their sale is to pay for your fines." "Larry, Larry!" she called. The children's father came running, but there was nothing he could do — the constables had pointed their muskets at his breast.

The constables thereupon dragged the weeping children toward the Salem harbor wharves where the square-rigged ships that sailed to foreign ports were docked. In a nearby ale house they located two rough, tough sea captains.

"Here, Captains, are two young religious devils we want you to sell as slaves in some distant port," the constables said. "And pray thee, you pompous landlubbers, by whose orders are we to sell this girl and this boy into slavery?" demanded the captains.

"By order of the magistrates of the General Court of the Massachusetts Bay Colony," the constables answered.

Rough men of the sea though they were, the captains were touched by the tears of the flaxen-haired girl and the near-defiance of the boy as they stood there with their agonized parents behind them. Setting his glass of ale down hard on the bar, the older captain, his face growing redder by the second, bellowed: "Go tell your old sour-faced magistrates that we order them to give these kids back to their parents." With that, the younger captain said to the constables: "Take your hands off that girl, and you, take your hands off that boy. Now, children, go home with your father and mother." And turning to the empty-handed constables, he added, "And now, tell the Court that if they ever try this again, we'll report the matter to King Charles when we reach England."

After this attack upon his business partner, Obadiah Holmes said: "I've had enough. I'll not take any more of this. Roger Williams and John Clarke are better off in the wilderness. I'll move to Newport and join up with Dr. Clarke, and I'll resist with all my might these hellish shackles upon the soul's liberty."

Now these two men, Clarke and Holmes, became great friends. They were men of iron will, strong in their love of liberty, and yet tenderhearted. Dr. Clarke would sit up all night with a patient to wait out the crisis of a fever. He would walk miles through the deep forest to reach the cabin of a poor pioneer whose wife was having a baby. He did double duty on these trips, for he brought in one hand medicine and healing, and in the other hand the Bible and prayer. Obadiah Holmes always stood by his friend, and during the years when Clarke was in England obtaining the charter for the colony, Holmes served as the pastor of the Baptist Church in Newport.

In Newport, one hot July day in 1651, Holmes said to his friend Clarke: "I've been thinking about poor brother William Witter up there in Lynn, Mass., where he is shut off from fellow Baptists and is surrounded by Puritans who hate his Baptist principles. We ought to visit him and encourage him."

"Well, don't forget it's a long walk. Eighty miles up there and eighty miles back in this suffocating July heat," answered Clarke.

"Yes, I know," said Holmes, "but also I know you well enough to know that the minute I remind you that he is aged and blind, you'll be on your way before I can say 'Jack Rabbit.'"

With that Clarke instantly pulled himself up to his full six feet of height. "Bring your Bible, your knapsack, and your gun. We'll need corn and molasses to eat, and the gun might get us a wolf or a bear or save us from some hostile Indian. Let's be off." They took with them another Baptist, John Crandall.

What did they talk about on their long hike through the forest? Well, there was Henry Dunster, the first president of Harvard College. After fourteen years of faithful service, the Grand Jury had compelled him to resign. Why? Because he had dared to preach against infant baptism, and because he had refused to have his own baby christened! Oh, there was plenty to talk about, what with all the sharp sayings of none too discreet Baptists and the trials and persecution carried on by the Puritan magistrates.

"It was worth that long, hot walk just to see the heavenly joy on Brother Witter's face when we told him who we were," said Holmes some weeks after they had returned to Newport.

"Indeed it was," said Clarke, "but look at all you suffered on the trip."

"Why, that — oh, that was to me like a garden of flowers in December," said Holmes.

"Well you ought to write that incident down for the sake of your grandchildren. Who knows but what someday your grandchildren may be famous," suggested Clarke. Little did he know how prophetic a remark he had made, for in very fact one of Obadiah Holmes' descendants was Abraham Lincoln. So here then is the true story of what happened 25 when they reached Lynn. They were conducting a Baptist service in Witter's home that July Sunday when constables entered, broke up the meeting, and arrested the three of them. The constables then forced them to attend the orthodox Puritan Church. Holmes, Clarke, and Crandall further enraged the constables by refusing to take off their hats in the meeting house, and Holmes still more by interrupting the sermon with a protest.

Dragged the ten miles from Lynn to Boston, all three were imprisoned for ten days before being brought to trial. The General Court convicted and sentenced them all, but Crandall was released. Holmes and Clarke were sentenced to pay fines or to be publicly "well-whipped." Both men refused on principle to pay fines when they had committed no evil. Accordingly, Clarke first was taken to the whipping post located on State Street near the center of the town, stripped of his clothing, and made ready for the laying on of the lashes. At this moment, the public humiliation of "a scholar, a gentleman, and a reverend divine in such a situation" proved too much for an unknown bystander. This bystander paid the fine and obtained Clarke's release before Clarke knew what had happened.

For some reason Holmes, as perhaps the more stubborn of the two Baptists, was kept in prison for over thirty days. Sympathizers tried to pay his fine, but he persistently refused to permit this. "I durst not accept of deliverance in such a way," he said.

By prayer, Holmes prepared himself for the ordeal. "When I heard the voice of my keeper come for me, every cheerfulness did come upon me and taking my Testament in hand I went along to the place of execution."

While they were stripping Holmes of his clothing at the whipping post, he said to the gathered crowd, "Now I find He does not fail me and therefore now I trust Him forever." Later he wrote of that hour's experience: "For in truth as the strokes fell upon me, I had such a spiritual manifestation of God's presence as the like thereof I had never had nor felt nor can with fleshly tongue so removed from me that indeed I am not able to declare it to you, . . . as the spectators said

the man striking with all his strength (Yea, spitting on his hands three times, as many affirmed) with a three-corded whip giving me thirty strokes."

Thirty strokes with a three-corded whip was equivalent to ninety strokes in all. As a result of this belaboring, the flesh of Holmes' back was reduced to jelly.

But what Holmes said to his persecutors when the whipping was over and done is a gem of Baptist history. Holmes wrote: "When he had loosed me from the post . . . having joyfulness in my heart . . . I told the magistrates, 'You have struck me with roses.' "

Yet even so, the roses made his back bleed, and afterward he suffered extreme pain. For days without number he could not sleep except as he rested on his knees and elbows, for his back and sides were too raw and sensitive for any part of his body to touch the bed. Even to befriend Holmes was to be arrested and fined. Because John Hazel and John Spur shook hands with him, they were promptly arrested and fined for their act. Baptists were denied many of the rights of citizenship, and they were subject to arrest, fines, prison, and the whipping post.

But it is of such heroic stuff that our Baptist forefathers were made. If blood tells, then something of this love of freedom and this resistance to all slavery was bequeathed by Holmes by lineal descent to our greatest President. The Obadiah Holmes family and the Samuel Lincoln family had been neighbors in Salem, Mass. It is no surprise, therefore, that in later years their grandchildren fell in love and married, and so it happened that Mordecai Lincoln II married the granddaughter of Obadiah Holmes. And don't forget that this Mordecai whom she married was the great-great grandfather of Abraham Lincoln. Thus, in the Lincoln family line there were Baptists who had drunk deeply from the spring of freedom. Lincoln's father, Thomas Lincoln, was not "shiftless," as has been falsely reported. He helped establish the Pigeon Creek Baptist Church in Indiana and served as the church moderator.

Was something of the spirit of Holmes bequeathed in the family blood and tradition of the Lincolns? One hears again

Lincoln's great second inaugural address in which he sees the scourge of war as God's judgment "until every drop of blood drawn with the lash shall be paid with another drawn with the sword," and feels again that ancient resistance to bondage, whether of mind or body. In any event, we ought never to forget that Lincoln's forbears and family were Baptists, and that Lincoln's upbringing was that of a frontier Baptist. Obadiah Holmes and Abraham Lincoln, each in his own time, held forth the great Baptist principles of liberty and freedom of conscience.

John Clarke and Obadiah Holmes

CHAPTER 3

JOHN BUNYAN

The Tinker Hero

"MIDNIGHT TONIGHT," they whispered to certain persons met on the village street and in doorways. "Midnight," they said in soft voices; "down by Duck Mill Lane, under the big elm tree on the Ouse River."

"You be a watcher against the coming of the constables," they appointed others. "Stand by the meadow-gate beyond the woods and whistle low if you see informers or constables approaching."

This secret meeting in the dead of night may sound like a robbers' rendezvous, but it was not. It was the way Baptists in the time of John Bunyan had to gather at secret "baptizing places" throughout England, especially during the reign of Charles the Second. But even before the persecutions under that king, Baptists were unpopular and subject to suspicion and opposition by the local authorities and the clergy of the established church. Baptists, therefore, often assembled in small groups by night for their baptismal services. Darkness offered protection.

In 1653, a twenty-eight-year-old tinker (or tinsmith) by the name of John Bunyan, was led into the water to be buried with Christ in baptism in the river close to Bedford.

And let me tell you, it was a great event that night when they baptized John Bunyan. For two and a half years he had been fighting his way up through doubts and fears and a sense of guilt and despair, until he came at last to a clear faith and great joy in serving Christ.

30

He had been a sport-loving youth, wrestling, bowling, racing, jumping, but "belching out oaths like a madman." "The very ringleader" of the town's youth "in all manner of vice and ungodliness," he confessed. Even a low character in the town shocked him one day by saying, "You're the ungodliest fellow for swearing I ever heard in all my life." But now everything was different. John Bunyan rose from the baptismal waters a new man fully surrendered to Christ. He had come a long way through heartrending struggles. Now Christ had a self-sacrificing and powerful witness in John Bunyan. Not long after his baptism, the good church members of Bedford suggested to Bunyan that he ought to preach. He hesitated. Despite his good looks, with his auburn hair and ruddy countenance, he was only an uneducated tinsmith, who had often peddled through the streets of the town of Bedford crying:

John Bunyan

"Have you any work for a tinker?

Have you any old bellows to mend?"

But preach Bunyan did, and when he preached the people listened entranced. They risked arrest to hear him preach, whether in the woods, in barns, in the open air, in secret homes, anywhere that they could quickly gather and disperse before the constables could break up the meeting. As he grew famous in later years, 3,000 people would gather early in the morning in London to listen to his preaching. He was different from the other preachers of his time. He was on fire for God. "I preached," he said, "what I did feel — what I did smartingly feel under which my poor soul did groan and tremble." Bunyan electrified his hearers, for he spoke with the earnestness of "one sent from the dead."

But the magistrates of the king and the jealous clergy of the Church of England said, "We'll put a stop to this mender of pots and pans, meddling with souls." And soon they attempted to do so. One November day in 1660, a secret Baptist meeting was to be held in a farmhouse in a meadow surrounded by high trees. When John Bunyan, who was to preach, arrived, he was taken aback by the anxiety which marked the faces of the congregation gathered in the house. "A warrant is out for your arrest, Brother Bunyan," said

31

the leader. "You will certainly be sent to prison. If you will let us call off the meeting now, there will be time for you to escape before the constables get here and nothing will happen."

Bunyan left the house in deep thought. He took one turn around the outside of the farmhouse. He had a wife and family. Prison would be no fun. Could he not run away and be free to preach another day? It seemed reasonable to escape while he had the chance.

He dashed back into the farmhouse. In that moment the tall youth was somehow taller than all the rest of the company. His blue eyes glinted "like the blue of a candle flame." He shook the auburn locks that fell to his shoulders and framed his ruddy face bronzed with the wind and sun of the open air. He flashed his firm decision to the gathered church in the house. "By no means will I run away. I will not stir, neither will I have the meeting dismissed. Come now, be of good cheer. Let's not be daunted. Our cause is right. We need not be ashamed of it. To preach God's Word is so good a work, we shall be well rewarded if we suffer for it." His friends now knew that Bunyan was a man of defiant courage. But neither he nor they knew that for this heroic decision his reward would be prison walls closed around him for twelve long years.

As the leader had feared, the constables led him off to the waiting magistrate. But what charge could they bring against a man armed only with a Bible and an eloquent tongue? You may be sure the king's constables did not frighten Bunyan, for he defied them as they led him away. "If I were out of prison today, I would preach the gospel again tomorrow by the help of God." "You're a blasted, stubborn rogue," one of the constables shouted at him.

The indictment against Bunyan charged as his crime that he "hath devilishly and pertinaciously abstained from coming to church [i.e., the Church of England], and was a common upholder of unlawful meetings — to the great disturbance of the good subjects of this Kingdom, contrary to the laws of our Sovereign Lord, the King."

32   So Bunyan was led away and locked up in prison for three

months to see if he would at the end of that time agree to go to church (the Church of England, of course) and give up his preaching as an Independent and Baptist. Otherwise he would be banished from the realm and possibly might be hanged for good measure.

Of course, there were well-meaning friends who advised him to take it easy: "Just drop into church once on Sunday; then you will be free the rest of the time, and at least you can preach, if you confine it to individuals and hold no meetings." Even Bunyan may have found this a subtle temptation, for his wife had taken sick with shock at news of his imprisonment and thereby had lost her baby. If he did not yield, then he would spend twelve years behind prison walls — twelve of the best years of a man's life. Twelve years in the Bedford County Prison amid the dirt, the vermin, and the fetid stench of a cell located over a rat-infested dungeon.

Of all the hardships awaiting him, many of which he could not then fully know, the bitterest to endure would be the separation from his wife and children. Indeed, his deepest pain would be his separation from his blind daughter whom he loved more tenderly than anything in all the world. He was never sure but what this dear child's blindness was not punishment for the sins of his wild youth. This drew him to her with a poignant love.

From his prison, when he feared that death was about to be decreed for him, he wrote: "The parting from my wife and poor children hath been to me as the pulling of my flesh from my bones . . . also because I should have often brought to my mind the hardships, miseries, and wants my poor family was like to meet with should I be taken from them, especially my poor blind child who lays nearer to my heart than all else besides. Poor child, thought I, what sorrow art thou like to have for thy portion in this world. Thou must be beaten, suffer hunger, cold, nakedness, and a thousand calamities though I cannot now endure the wind should blow upon thee."

But the joke was on those who had tried to stop John Bunyan from preaching the gospel. God, as he has promised, works with those who love him to bring forth good out of even the things that seem against them. So it was in John Bunyan's case. During these prison years he had much time on his hands to think and to write down his thoughts. The tinker then became the thinker. Books and pamphlets poured from his pen and were read by thousands. He had a vivid imagination, he knew the language of the people, and he was a genius with his pen.

Like Paul and Luther, Bunyan, when shut away from the world outside, discovered how to describe the new and wonderful world inside each man. After long reflection and much practice in writing, toward the last part of his prison confinement he began to write a breath-taking story, an allegory, so vibrant with interest, so sparkling with realism, and so spiritually refreshing to readers that his publishers had to print a second edition of his book before the first year ended.

The book was called *The Pilgrim's Progress,* and one hundred thousand copies were soon sold — a tremendous sale for a book in the seventeenth century. His book was alive with lions and giants, with castles and maidens, with judges and juries, with Vanity Fair, the Pope, and humorous and serious characters that made it exciting reading. Among his most graphic characters are the fat and sleek Mr. Worldly Wiseman, the willowy Mr. Pliable, and the unreliable Mr. Facing Both Ways. Such has been the spiritual vitality of *The Pilgrim's Progress* that it has crossed the seven seas and all the continents. Today it has been translated into more languages than any other book except the Bible. It was first printed in February, 1678, by a London publisher whose name and address have a quaint English sound, "Nathaniel Ponder at the Peacock in the Poultry." The book has now maintained its popularity as a classic for two hundred and eighty-three years, placing the poor baptized tinker among the literary immortals. Though his pen was prolific and he wrote many books, sermons, and pamphlets, he always will be best known as the author of *The Pilgrim's Progress.*

By the simplicity, directness, and vividness with which he wrote, Bunyan gave the gospel widespread appeal. Thus, his prison years still enrich the world, for his book can be found under the midnight sun in Norway and under the hot sun of the African Congo. Its language and appeal are universal and its spiritual robustness is unsurpassed by any book except the Bible.

The Pilgrim's Progress has been printed in one hundred and forty-eight languages, which is only thirty short of the number of languages in which the complete Bible is now available. It appears in languages as distantly separated as Eskimo, Tibetan, and Fijian. The latest publishing of his book is in the language of the Tonga people of the Zambesi Valley in Africa. A presentation edition of Bunyan, recently published in London, in handsome white leather binding, was quickly sold out.

The artists who have made the illustrations for *The Pilgrim's Progress* have done so after the manner of their own country. In Japan, Pilgrim is a warrior of the Samurai type with a long sword and chain armor. In Borneo, the Sea Dyaks demanded a fierce looking Apollyon, while in Africa the illustrations of *The Pilgrim's Progress* show the characters dressed in bush shirt and shorts.

John Bunyan, who was always poor, would be astounded to know that more than thirty years ago a copy of the original edition of *The Pilgrim's Progress* sold for $30,000, and today is valued at $60,000. Even the warrant for Bunyan's arrest is now valued at $3,000.

One last mission closed the gates on the earthly pilgrimage of Bunyan. While ever an unyielding man of principle, he was also a beloved peacemaker. A young neighbor of his in Bedford had incurred the wrath of his father and there was bad blood between them. The father was resolved to disinherit his son. The son petitioned Bunyan to go to the father and effect a reconciliation. Bunyan was too tired to go, but like a good soldier he answered the call.

All that spring Bunyan had suffered severe influenza. He was in a decidedly weakened condition when he mounted his horse to go to Reading to see the irate father. That night, still worn and tired, he preached in the church in Reading. The next morning, pursuing his gracious mission, 35 he called on the father and broke the hardness of his heart. "All right, I will send for my son. I'll surely be glad to see him now."

Mission accomplished, Bunyan started back, riding the more than forty miles to London. A cloudburst of rain blinded his horse who frequently stumbled. The horse had to go slowly, leaving Bunyan to be even more drenched with the cold rain. Finally he reached London and put up at the home of his friend, John Strodwick. But he was so weak that he was scarcely able to alight from his jaded horse. Quickly his friends gave him hot drinks and tucked him in bed to end his chill and ease his aching bones.

Feeling slightly better the next day, he sat up in bed and finished writing his last book, *The Acceptable Sacrifice*. When Sunday came he insisted on keeping his engagement to preach in Whitechapel meeting house. From the pulpit, he came back to bed with a high fever. His once strong physique now was too much weakened by his long years in prison, his arduous labors, and his recent drenching ride from Reading, to recover from the strain of his illness. And so he passed over onto the other side of the river and all the bells of the city rang to welcome the Pilgrim.

Of all persecuted Baptists, Bunyan was longest in prison. Alone among Baptists, he obtained a place in literature with the immortals. Alone among Baptists, he produced a classic still widely read and treasured after nearly three hundred years. He embodied the Baptist emphasis upon a changed life — a new birth — by his turning away from sin and folly to a life of rare and unreserved dedication. Among our Baptist forefathers none was more uncompromising in principle and yet more broad-minded in fellowship. When he was tempted with offers of liberty from prison, if he would renounce his Baptist convictions, he said:

"I have determined the Almighty God being my help and shield, yet to suffer . . . even till the moss shall grow on mine eyebrows rather than thus to violate my Father and principles." Yet he was willing to fellowship with those unimmersed. Although himself a strong believing Baptist, he did not favor "making an idol of baptism." He let his own church in Bedford offer open membership to those who had failed to find for themselves the light on believer's immersion.

His love for Christ and his personal loyalty to him has not been surpassed: "I have loved to hear my Lord spoken of," he wrote, "and wherever I have seen the print of his shoes in the earth, there I have coveted to set my foot, too."

John Bunyan

And now even his soul must enjoy a quiet smile (he always had a fine sense of humor), for in the Church of England hymnbook, (the church which secured his long imprisonment and despised him as an ignorant ranter) one of his hymns has an honored place. So the clock turns round and God fulfills himself in many ways — even by making a poor tinker a literary immortal!

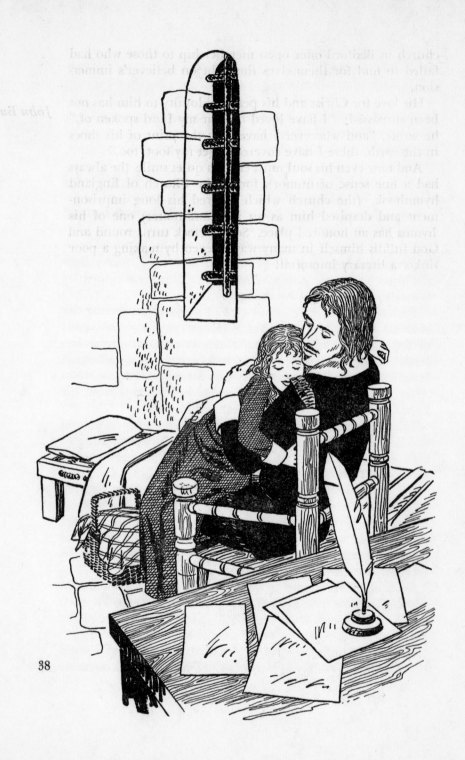

CHAPTER 4

JAMES IRELAND

Pioneer Virginia Baptist

IN VIRGINIA, between the years 1768 and 1777, thirty Baptist preachers were either thrown into prison, whipped by law officers, or stoned by mobs.

Perhaps the most infamous case of persecution during the colonial period, and one that is rather typical of the status of Baptists in Virginia at that time, was that of James Ireland. Though his name was Ireland, he was acually a bonnie Scotsman from Edinburgh. At first he was a Presbyterian. After he came to Virginia, however, he changed from his Presbyterian viewpoint and became a Baptist.

Like so many of the self-educated pioneer preachers among the Baptists at the time, he was a strong, independent, and even eccentric individual. He was afraid of no man, and he took orders from no one but God.

He made use of his canny Scotch cleverness in fighting off his persecutors. For example, he was warned on one occasion that if he preached in a certain Mr. Manifa's house, he would be arrested by the squire and Mr. Manifa would be fined twenty pounds for permitting his property to be used for preaching by the Baptists.

Ireland cleverly got around this threat. He asked Mr. Manifa to show him the boundary line of his land. He then had a table placed across it, with two legs on one side of the line and two legs on the other side of the line.

To Mr. Manifa, he gave this explanation: "When I stand on this table, I shall not be preaching on your land anymore

than on another's." This, of course, was a calculated device
to confuse the old squire in regard to the question of whose
land he was really preaching on and who therefore was really
the guilty person.

This trick, so far as avoiding arrest was concerned, did
not work. But with respect to getting a large congregation,
it did work. It was something new to see a preacher standing
on a table on a boundary line, waving his arms and shouting
in a loud voice.

Ireland himself has described what happened: "Preaching
being over and concluding with a prayer, I heard a rustling
noise in the woods and before I could open my eyes to see
who it was, I was seized by the collar by two men while
standing on the table — they told me that I must give security not to teach, preach, or exhort for twelve months and a
day or I must go to jail. . . . I have security to attend court
. . . which I accordingly did. . . . There were eleven magistrates who sat as a quorum. They browbeat me . . . would
admit of no defense I could make, but ordered me to hold
my tongue and let them hear no more of my vile, pernicious,
abhorrible, detestable, abominable, diabolical doctrines, for
they were nauseous to the whole court. . . . I delivered up
my riding horse for a friend to take care of. . . . The sheriffs
were ordered to attend me to my little limbo [jail] with a
considerable parade of people with such volleys of oaths and
abuse as if I were being unfit to exist on the earth . . . sticks
and stones they were throwing the whole night upon me."

It happened that the man who kept the jail also kept the
town tavern. He threw his drunks into jail with Ireland
where they often roundly abused the preacher. On the other
hand, if any Baptists wanted to visit Ireland, they had to
pay four shillings and eight pence for the privilege. The
jailer discovered that it was rather profitable financially to
keep Ireland behind bars.

Ireland, however, was so magnetic in personality that the
people could not stay away from his jail. Crowds gathered
under his barred window and the keen Ireland saw the opportunity to make his jail a unique pulpit. He preached
through the bars of a window to the people who gathered

40

outside. Naturally, the bishop and the Anglican priest, as well as the sheriff and the squire, were furious with anger.

Ireland reported: "When I would be preaching through the little iron grate, the wicked and the persecutors would ride up at a gallop among my listeners, until Negroes were stripped and subjected to stripes and myself threatened with being shut up in total darkness if ever I presumed to preach to the people again."

There was no end of attempts to make life miserable for Ireland. So low-minded was the mob at Culpeper that more than once, when he attempted to preach, they heaped indescribable indignities upon him.

Once an attempt was made to blow up the jail, but the explosion lacked sufficient powder and no damage was done to Ireland himself, except that the loud noise of the explosion suddenly ended his hymn singing.

His tormentors next put Indian red pepper and brimstone in the open space where the jail door was a few inches above the doorsill. By setting fire to the pepper and brimstone they filled Ireland's cell with "killing smoke." But this tough Scotsman said that he put his mouth to the cracks and drew in fresh air in order to prevent his suffocation.

One more attempt was made upon his life when the jailer and the doctor conspired to poison Ireland. The poison made him seriously ill, and generous Baptists raised two hundred pounds to release Ireland and put him under a good doctor's care, but Ireland refused to leave the jail under such circumstances.

Ireland was permitted to write letters, however, and during the five months he was in jail he wrote many letters to fellow Baptists. Characteristic of his optimistic nature, he put in his letters as a salutation, "From My Palace in Culpeper."

Ireland's cleverness was clearly marked by his conduct at his trial. Again he succeeded in confusing the judges. When his lawyer finally proved that Ireland's imprisonment had been illegal, the judges and the magistrates one by one walked off the bench and Ireland automatically became a free man.

Ireland was widely heard because he not only possessed a fascinating Scotch accent, but also had a commanding personality and a resonant voice as a preacher. He had the old-world eloquence of the orator and the tremendous energy of the pioneer. Being so popular a preacher, it is not surprising that he incurred the jealousy of the Episcopal preachers of the established church in Virginia. Naturally they wanted to put him to silence.

The boldness of Ireland helped to end the persecution of Baptists in Virginia. Today, in the tower of the First Baptist Church of Culpeper, Va., there hangs a bell which bears this inscription:

To the Memory
of
James Ireland
Born in 1748, died in 1806

As early as 1661, the Church of England had become so firmly established in Virginia that it could compel every citizen to attend church every Sunday under penalty of fifty pounds of tobacco. A few years later everyone was taxed to support the clergymen of the Church of England.

A statute promulgated in 1662 was very hard on the Baptists, for it stipulated that a penalty of two thousand pounds of tobacco should be assessed on any father who refused to have his child baptized in the Church of England.

Just as in New England, Henry Dunster, the first president of Harvard, was forced to resign for refusing to have his child christened, so John Briggs in lower Norfolk County, Va., had to pay a penalty of three thousand, two hundred and twenty-five pounds of tobacco for refusing to have his children christened.

At long last, however, through the courage of men like James Ireland, and later by means of the Bill of Rights written into the Constitution, Baptists became possessed of absolute freedom of worship. The Baptists now are the strongest religious body in the state of Virginia.

CHAPTER 5

ISAAC BACKUS

Horseman of Liberty

HE HAD JUST TURNED SIXTEEN — this healthy New England farm boy, born January 9, 1724 — tall, strong-muscled, and deep-bronzed by wind and sun. He tossed his shirt over a bush on the edge of the hayfield and gripped the handles of his scythe firmly. He was working on the farm of his father, Samuel Backus, part owner of the Backus Iron Works. It was mid-August and haying time again. The sun was blazing mercilessly, and streams of sweat trickled down the boy's bare chest and back. He swung his scythe in wide, sweeping arcs. The sharp edge of the scythe sang as it cut the breeze and felled the tall grasses.

Something was on the mind of young Isaac Backus. He swung the scythe with a more fierce energy, as if by force to free his mind from troublesome thoughts. The smell of the sweet white and purple clover only aggravated his restless brooding. Just ahead, and in the path of his scythe, was a clump of white and yellow daisies. His scythe cut down the bright blooming flowers. They fell limp and flat in death. Through his mind came unexpectedly the words: "Man is as the flower of the field. Today he flourisheth, tomorrow he is cut down and withereth." Suddenly Isaac halted his scythe in mid-air. Then slowly he lifted its long wooden upright to his shoulder. He walked with measured steps over to the bordering stone wall and sat down under a cool-shading oak. It was time to wrestle with his disturbing problem. He could not put it off any longer.

43

What was on his mind was indeed serious. A great revival of religion was arousing all New England. George White-field of England had been giving the call to surrender to Christ with eloquent and moving appeal. Young Isaac Backus had been stirred by the new spirit of religious fervor which had been awakened in the area of Norwich, Conn.

As he meditated under the tree on his spiritual condition, he saw himself "a hardened sinner." In the revival meetings he had come to see how much he needed the Savior.

This quiet hour of reflection and decision came to a glorious consummation when he fell upon his knees and in an earnest and heartfelt prayer surrendered to Christ. What took place on that hot summer's day in 1740 is best described in his own words: "My soul yielded all into His hands, fell at His feet, and was silent and calm before Him. . . . The Word of God and the promises of His grace appeared firmer than a rock, and I was astonished at my previous unbelief. My heavy burden was gone, tormenting fears were fled, and my joy was unspeakable."

Yet even after his conversion, his inner spirit was still uncertain because he had not had a more spectacular or excitingly emotional religious experience. Fortunately, on the following Sunday, he heard a sermon which helped to assure him that his conversion was genuine. He found that the best evidences of a changed life were the five things he was now realizing in his own life, namely, "a spirit of prayer, hatred of sin, overcoming of the world, love to the brethren, and love to enemies."

Although young Backus became a member of the Congregational Church in Norwich, he did not long remain happy in that church. His spirit craved a church where a real conversion was preached as essential to true Christian living.

Sometime after this, a call sounded in the soul of this young man. "A conviction seized my mind," he wrote, "that God had given me abilities which his church had a right to the use of and which I could not withhold with a clear conscience."

Once more it was in a quiet time at the edge of the woods that he meditated and prayed. Here his call to preach be-

44

came clear and powerful. Though he then was only twenty-two years old, he felt so certain of his new calling that he preached on the following Sunday. The people in the little congregation also felt certain that he was truly a man chosen and called of God to preach the gospel.

Traveling by horseback through southern New England and preaching as occasion offered opportunity, he came at last to a Separate Congregational church in Middleborough, Mass., which called him as its pastor.

Two surprises were in store for Backus and this church. First, he would remain there as pastor for more than fifty years, becoming during that time nationally famous; and second, he would lead some of the members of that church to join him in forming, on January 16, 1756, a Baptist church — the Middleborough Baptist Church.

But Isaac Backus had not taken up Baptist beliefs quickly or easily. In 1749 he had begun a study of the doctrine of baptism. For two full years he struggled with the problem of whether or not the Bible taught infant baptism. It was not until August 22, 1751 that he and six members of his church entered the water to be baptized.

Out of his soul-searching studies and his revulsion at the persecution of preachers who did not conform to the standing church in New England (i.e., the Congregational), he came to clearly defined convictions respecting the rights of conscience and freedom of belief. The weak, abused, and persecuted Baptists of the New England area now found in this young minister their stoutest champion. He leaped into the forefront of the battle for liberty of religious faith.

Thus, at about the same time that the American colonies were stirring with claims to freedom from the unjust taxes imposed by England, the energetic Backus was lifting aloft the torch of religious liberty. And, indeed, there was great need for such a crusader for the rights of conscience.

From his youth, Backus had seen men arrested, imprisoned, and their property confiscated, because they could not in good conscience pay taxes forced upon them to support a church in which they did not believe. He knew the hour had struck to support religious freedom.

Indeed, his zeal for religious liberty had grown out of personal experience. He had seen his mother, Elizabeth Backus, one of the revival converts of the Great Awakening, taken to jail on a bitter October night and held prisoner for nearly two weeks. Later, he himself, because he had refused to separate himself from this revival movement, had been fined and imprisoned. He was not released until a friend paid for him the fine which he had refused to pay.

In Ashfield, Mass., nearly four hundred acres of land belonging to the Baptists had been sold and the money used as religious taxes to help build a Congregational Church.

Aroused by events like these, a group of Baptist churches combined their interests in what was called the Warren Association. They appointed Backus as their official agent to travel about and fight in behalf of religious liberty the rights of Baptists wherever there might be need. The Warren Association chose well, for Backus became "one of the most two-fisted, hard-fighting Yankees the Colonies ever reared."

Carrying out his work as the agent of the Warren Association, Backus rode horseback to present a petition for Baptist liberties to the First Continental Congress. Failing of success in this first Philadelphia visit, Isaac Backus drew up a memorial petition on behalf of the Baptist churches and presented it to the Provincial Congress which met in Cambridge, Mass., on December 9, 1774.

Again he presented a memorial petition to the Colonial Assembly when it convened at Watertown, Mass., in July 1775. There was no mincing of words in these memorials. Backus was a tough fighter when it came to standing fast for liberty for all Americans.

Backus was the able draftsman of these various Baptist memorials and he was soon known as the champion of nonconformity in New England.

He needed courage when he waited on the Congress in Philadelphia. He was rebuffed by the committee of the Congress and vilified in the press. Newspaper articles roundly abused him. In one he was threatened with "a halter and the gallows." His life could have been in danger. "The undaunted intrepidity with which he withstood corrupt or

47

party-blinded judges, even to the face," was long remembered by many of his contemporaries.

The need to insist upon absolute liberty and to defend the rights of Baptists was illustrated at one time by what happened in the town of Pepperel, forty miles from Boston.

A small company of Baptists had gathered by the river to baptize six candidates. A mob gathered and baptized a dog in the river in derision of the little company of Baptists. The believers then went to another location in the town beside another river, but the mob followed. Here two dogs were dipped in the river in ridicule, and one young man dipped yet another dog in the river in scorn and derision of the Baptists.

Feeling was now running so high that the officers of the town advised the Baptist ministers to depart immediately out of the town for their own safety. They were in danger of their lives. In consequence, the Baptists dispersed to meet again secretly, and "those six persons were baptized, after which the mob offered them some further abuse." Thus the Baptists needed a champion like Backus to secure their liberties and their rights.

Though he was an uneducated man, his ability as a preacher, as a defender of liberty, and as a writer were widely recognized. Various Baptist leaders pressed him to write a history of the churches of New England. As a matter of fact, he finally responded with three notable volumes which are still esteemed by historians. But at the time, he wrote: "When I was requested by several gentlemen of note and others to undertake this work, two great objections presented themselves to my mind. Namely, my great unfitness for it and the difficulty of obtaining the necessary materials. But their importunity prevailed against the first and Divine Providence has removed the other by conveying into my hands a variety of authentic materials much beyond what I could have foreseen could have now been obtained in the world." In all, Backus history contains 1,300 pages.

His fame and abilities spread far among Baptists, and churches in the South asked for his assistance in Virginia and North Carolina. He spent six months in those states, traveling over 3,000 miles on horseback and preaching over 126 sermons.

In addition to his wide travels and his three historical volumes, he wrote over forty other publications, chiefly sermons and pamphlets, not to mention circular letters and articles in various periodicals.

He served for sixty years as a minister of the gospel and only laid down his burdens when he had reached the venerable age of eighty-three. He finished his earthly course in New England on November 20, 1806.

A beautiful anecdote is told of Isaac Backus which indicates the quality of his spiritual life. Two New England Baptist preachers had quarreled and all efforts at reconciliation had failed. Finally three notable Baptist ministers were brought together in conference, along with others, in the effort to end the quarrel between the two. The hours of the night passed away slowly and there was no indication of a breakdown toward reconciliation. Finally, when it was almost time for the dawn, Isaac Backus, who had appeared to be only partly listening, said as he stood up, "Let us look to the throne of grace once more." Then, kneeling down, he prayed. The spirit and tone of his prayer were such as to make everyone feel that the heart-searching God had come down among them. The result was that the hearts of the contending parties began immediately to melt and the rising sun saw the rupture healed and closed up forever.

One of those who heard him pray said: "I have often heard that good man pray. The efficacy of his prayers did not consist in length nor gaudy dress; but it seemed that he and his God loved one another, and that he was at home before the throne of grace."

Yes, Isaac Backus and his God loved one another, and so it was that quietly he slipped home to be with God.

Mecklin, a Dartmouth historian, has said: "Isaac Backus belongs to every age and to all men who love liberty. Backus alone deserves to be called the worthy successor of Roger Williams and John Clarke in the long, long struggle for religious liberty."

CHAPTER 6

WILLIAM CAREY

The Uncommon Common Man

"HI THERE, Columbus! Come over here!"

In answer to the shout, Columbus, with two other boys, ran panting across a field at the edge of the village of Paulerspury, England. They joined a group of friends who were hunched in a circle about some object on the ground.

"What kind of insect is this?" one lad demanded. "We found it under a log."

"Yes, Columbus, you know all about bugs. Tell us what's the name of this one."

Columbus knelt, scooped up the bug in his hand, examined it closely, screwed up his face, and admitted: "This is a new one to me. Come on over to my room, and I'll look it up in a book."

This invitation was just what the boys had hoped for. With a whoop, they followed Columbus down the village street toward his home, near the school.

His name, of course, was not really Columbus. That was the nickname his playmates had given him because he was forever reading a biography of Christopher Columbus, and because he talked incessantly about the lands far away across the sea. Columbus suited him far better than plain Bill Carey, his own name.

As they scuffed the mud from their shoes on the iron scrapper at Bill's house, the boys overheard a neighbor woman talking to his mother inside.

50   "Well, a boy's bedroom, I say, ought to be a boy's bed-

room. Land's sake, it's scandalous — having all those birds and bugs and butterflies all over Bill's room! Why, you can't step inside, hardly, it's so crowded. I wouldn't let my Jonathan turn his bedroom into a bughouse, I'll tell you that!"

Mrs. Carey's voice was patient. "William's father encourages him to gather specimens of insects and birds, and I just feel that he's a boy only once. I'd rather have him do that than run the streets and get into mischief."

"Well, he's your boy. If you want his room to be a cage for wild creatures, I guess it's your business."

She was preparing to leave. The boys waited outside the door, exchanging eloquent glances.

Presently she appeared, gave them a look that asked plainly, "Well, what now?" Then, lifting her skirts, she hurried sputtering down the flagstone walk, and away.

She was not far wrong in her description of young William Carey's bedroom. It was a live aviary, an insectarium, and a small botanical garden combined.

Bill had a passion for living creatures and growing things. He knew the name of every bird, butterfly, insect, and flower to be found for miles around. He was a walking encyclopedia of natural history. He was constantly learning more, for he spent his spare time inspecting the brooks and the lush meadows that curved upward from the village of Paulerspury, in the Midlands of England.

There, on August 17, 1761, William Carey had been born, and there he spent his all too brief boyhood. For a poor village lad in England, in those days, play days and school days were soon ended.

Overseas, in the American colonies, the French and Indian War had ended in 1763. Carey then had been just two years old. Colonel George Washington had just passed his thirtieth birthday, and was not yet a general.

So the day came when the young Carey, fourteen years of age, said good-by to Paulerspury and his lively companions, and hiked away to Piddington to learn the shoemaker's trade and to begin work as an apprentice.

His friends, momentarily sobered, watched him go, a small figure in a blue coat, buff-colored waistcoat, leather breeches, 51 speckled stockings, and scuttle hat. The bundle he carried on his back contained pitifully little besides his beloved *Life of Columbus,* a package of seeds, and a Latin book, for he had developed a great passion for the study of languages.

Far down the village street he turned, waved once more, and disappeared.

"Young Carey, you will work beside John Warr," the taskmaster's loud voice ordered. "He's three years older than you, so see to it that you pay attention to the way he cuts and sews the leather."

As if pegging shoes in poverty for long hours each day and sleeping at night in the attic were not rugged enough, Bill was plagued with a hard taskmaster, one Clarke Nichols. The boy tried to take comfort in the books he kept beside his workbench, his *Life of Columbus* and his Latin book.

But the hot temper and cursing tongue of Clarke Nichols, together with his drunken rages and unreasonable demands, often discouraged the poor young apprentice. He himself fell to swearing at times, and lying, as he had in Paulerspury when he had disobeyed his father by keeping bad company.

One influence, however, steadied him. Bill liked John Warr. John Warr liked Bill and was determined to lead him to Christ. He did lead him as far as prayer meeting at the church, but Bill was not ready as yet to go farther.

A crisis came one Christmas when Bill cheated his master by passing off on him a counterfeit shilling. His crime was detected. He feared dismissal, arrest, and disgrace.

Probably the taskmaster's wife interceded for young Bill. Anyhow, he was mercifully forgiven.

Nevertheless, his burst of dishonesty frightened him. It suddenly made him see himself as a sinner in need of a forgiving Savior. Slowly, gradually, he came to believe in Christ as his great Redeemer.

Young Carey knew that an overcoming power had now entered his life. It was like a new beginning or a new birth, yet he never could point to any particular day or hour when this had decisively happened. For him it had been a long struggle and a growing experience.

52   Largely it was John Warr who won the seventeen-year-old

Bill to Christ, even as Andrew, centuries before, had won his own brother, Peter. Carey was to write, "Under John Warr's influence, I determined to leave off lying, swearing, and other sins."

No longer did he want to burn down the Meeting House at Hackleton, where prayer meetings were held by those who would not go to the Anglican (Episcopal) church, in which he had been brought up. No longer, as formerly, did he scorn and disdain the humble Independents and Baptists.

During this time of spiritual searching, many religious people tried to persuade Carey to adopt their sectarian beliefs. He became confused, and in seeking the answers, he was led to continue his study of Greek and also to take up Hebrew.

Thus, while he carried on his business of cobbling shoes, "he pressed God's lamp close to his breast."

Friends were always drawn to young Carey, and two ministers who became friendly with him helped him in his understanding of the gospel. They were Thomas Scott of Olney and Thomas Skinner of Clipston.

Skinner loaned Carey a book entitled *Help to Zion's Travelers*, by Robert Hall the elder, a Baptist. Carey had never before read a book which gave him such rapture. To him this book was "sweetest wine." The viewpoint of Hall served to confirm the beliefs into which Carey's own studies of the Scriptures were leading him.

In his heart he knew that he ought to crucify his pride as an Anglican and join himself to the despised Baptists, "outside the camp" of prideful respectability.

While he wavered, God used a king to bring about His will. Across the seas, the American Revolution was in progress. King George III of Britain was worried about the failure of the British army and navy to subdue the Colonies. He, therefore, made February 10, 1779, to be a day of national fasting and prayer in England.

John Warr took young William Carey to spend this day of worship in the Hackleton Meeting House. There, a lay preacher pleaded for full dedication to Christ, using the text: "Let us go forth therefore unto him without the camp, 53 bearing his reproach." This text pierced Carey's conscience.

Then, a sermon railing against the Baptist beliefs spurred him into action. Sure at last of his convictions, he applied for baptism according to the Scriptures.

Up at dawn one October morning in the year 1783, William Carey walked five miles to the Nene River in order to be in time for his baptism by Dr. John Ryland at six o'clock.

Since the young man was but a poor village shoemaker and the only candidate, none but a handful of the most faithful came to witness the event. The church recorded no particular elation over this lonely morning immersion of a poor journeyman cobbler. Yet this baptismal hour, which seemed to mean so little, meant much to Carey, and it came to mean much to many the wide world over.

By now, Carey was a shoemaker on his own in the village of Moulton, where he preached at the little Baptist church on Sunday and taught charity school in off-hours.

In his low-ceilinged room in the cottage at Moulton, Carey welcomed a visitor one morning.

He was hard at work in the bright bay window when the voice greeted him. "Good morning, Brother Carey."

Carey rose hastily, at the same time taking the shoe nails out of his mouth. "Mr. Gotch! Good morning!" He brushed his leather apron, quickly. "May I serve you?"

"I have another order for you," the visitor told him. "The army needs ten pairs of boots, size 10, by next Saturday night a week. Can you get them for me?"

"You shall have them and on time," Carey promised.

Their business done, Gotch looked about the room. "I see you have English daisies in your window."

"Yes. They are my favorite flower, sir."

"And what's that on the wall beyond your workbench, a world map?"

Carey nodded. "I have made the continents in color, as you see. Also, I have penned upon the margin some chosen facts about many parts of the world."

Gotch's answer was an echo from the old days in Paulerspury. "You've got the spirit of a Columbus."

Next his visitor's eye was caught by a round object on the

workbench. He examined it. "A bright colored globe, made of stitched leather! I have never seen one like this!"

Carey explained. "The charity school had no money to buy a globe, so I made this one by sewing leather pieces together like a soccer ball. Then I colored the continents and the oceans so that it would interest the children."

As he listened, Gotch had picked up a book printed in strange characters. "What in tarnation is this?" he asked.

"A Hebrew Old Testament, sir," Carey said modestly.

His eyes wide with surprise, Gotch exclaimed, "I saw your Greek Testament over there on the bench, but I didn't know you read Hebrew too."

Carey's reply was very simple. "It is a great help in my Bible study."

Gotch paced back and forth across the room, glancing at Carey now and then with an appraising eye. At length he said, "Carey, when you deliver those shoes at my shop in Kettering next Saturday, I have something to say to you."

With that, he went out and shut the door.

William Carey found it impossible to keep his mind upon his work that day.

He had displeased Mr. Gotch, he was sure. His employer considered the language study and the map making a waste of time. Because of them, the work upon the shoes had been inferior. That must be it. He would lose his job.

All that week he tended to his cobbling, and dreaded Saturday.

But Saturday came and in the evening Carey, with inner trembling, loaded the heavy pack of shoes upon his back and walked the twelve miles to Kettering.

There in Gotch's shop he set down the bundle and opened the sack. "Here are your shoes, Mr. Gotch." He waited, scarcely daring to breathe.

Gotch looked the shoes over and spoke: "See here, Carey. I don't mean you to spoil any more of my leather."

The heart of William Carey sank. Shoemaking was his only trade. His preacher's salary was not enough even to buy him clothes. Without work, how could he support his wife and children?

Gotch studied him sharply. "How much money do you make in a week of cobbling shoes?"

Carey managed to say fearfully, "I earn about nine or ten shillings, sir."

"All right, then." Suddenly a twinkle shone in Gotch's eyes. "Suppose hereafter you concentrate on your Latin, Greek, Hebrew, French, and Dutch, and I'll give you a weekly allowance of ten shillings so that you'll be free to pursue your studies."

Carey was stunned. He could scarcely believe his ears. His eyes filled, and in a trembling voice he whispered an understatement. "I — I'm taken back with amazement. And — and gratitude. Thank you, Mr. Gotch! Thank you!"

Well might countless thousands echo, "Thank you, Mr. Gotch! Thank you!" For this shrewd businessman had discerned in the humble cobbler and village pastor a future greatness as yet undreamed of, a gift that might have been buried in the little cobbler's shop in Moulton forever.

Now that Carey was preaching as a pastor, a crucial question arose: Would the Baptists ordain him? It looked doubtful. They debated the problem for a year. Carey was instructed to preach three trial sermons, while they weighed the matter. At last they agreed upon his ordination.

Carey was so poor that he had no decent suit of clothes in which to be ordained. A devoted church member, a certain Miss Tressler, went from door to door begging money to outfit the poverty-stricken preacher for the occasion.

A recognized minister at last, and one known for his mastery of languages, Carey preached in open Baptist gatherings the radical ideas he had formerly proposed only in private and group conversations.

From reading Cooke's *Travels,* and more particularly from his study of the Bible, he had reached the strong conviction that Christians in England ought to send missionaries to the heathen.

However, there was serious doubt as to Carey's good judgment when he proposed that Baptists should stir up their sleeping energies and carry the gospel to the heathen world. Once, at an open meeting, he was sternly rebuked for his

rash notion by no other than the influential Dr. John Ryland, who had baptized him.

"Sit down, young man. When the Lord gets ready to convert the heathen he will do it without your help or mine,"
declared Dr. Ryland.

But Carey could not be silenced. Would God indeed ask
a poor shoemaker to go forth from his English village and
storm the barred gates of heathendom? But no doubt lodged
in the mind of the man who was to be known as the father
of modern missions, who was to pioneer a new trail for all
Christendom. His vision was clear. His determination was
undaunted.

His chance came when he preached at a meeting of Baptist delegates from many churches. Carey challenged the
churches to break open the narrow cocoon of self-confine-
ment and wing out into a wider world with the message of
the saving gospel.

"Lengthen your cords and strengthen your stakes," he
pleaded, as he painted vivid pictures of the superstition,
suffering, and ignorance of the multimillion heathen to
whom no one offered the compassion of Christ.

He rose in simple eloquence to a climax, the words of
which are forever burned into the Christian conscience.

"Expect great things from God. Attempt great things for
God."

At last his message stirred thirteen people to meet on the
night of October 2, 1792, in the home of Mrs. Beebe Wallis,
in Kettering. There in a room only ten by twelve feet in
size was organized the first foreign missionary society of
modern times. The few who were present pledged about
$37.00 to finance the work.

The leading spirit behind the movement was Carey's great
friend and supporter, the pastor of the Baptist Church in
Kettering, the Reverend Andrew Fuller.

"We'll hold the ropes, William, if you'll go to India,"
promised Fuller. "On that day," says A. C. Underwood,
"Baptists were leading the whole church of Christ." "A new
era in Protestant missions began with Carey," declares Ken-
neth Scott Latourette.

There were many discouraging roadblocks, however, but the day finally came when Carey, sustained more by faith than by an assured security behind him, sailed for Calcutta, India.

It was a stormy voyage. The little Danish ship was driven nearly to the coast of Brazil, and almost wrecked off the Cape of Good Hope. In all its voyage of five months, it never passed another ship, nor did it land at any port until it dropped anchor in the heat of the Calcutta harbor.

For William Carey there followed heartbreaking experiences of poverty almost to the point of starvation, of sickness in his family, and of the death of one of his children. Too, Carey faced the opposition of his own British government, which tried to stop all his missionary endeavors. Furthermore, the intellectual and literary leaders of England despised him. Sidney Smith, the editor of the highbrow *Edinburgh Review* — a magazine read by all the important people — sneered at him as "a consecrated cobbler, a delirious mechanic, and a didactic artisan."

For a time, it seemed that his great enterprise of faith must fizzle into failure. Carey, however, had too much perseverance to quit. Only death could stop him — and it almost did, for his wife became mentally deranged and attempted to take his life.

Because the meager support coming from England was not sufficient to provide for his family and fellow missionaries, Carey was forced to seek secular employment.

Besides the torment of his personal problems, Carey suffered great outrage of spirit at the sight of the cruelties inflicted in India upon the women and children.

At his desk in his house in Serampore, Carey's hand trembled with hot anger as he wrote his friend in England, Dr. John Ryland. He had just seen a young widow tied with bamboo poles on a pile of wood and burned alongside the body of her dead husband. Carey had tried in vain to stop this shocking murder.

He wrote: "They tied her down with bamboo poles and piled dry leaves high above her, pouring melted preserved butter on top. Fire was put to the pile which immediately blazed very fiercely. No sooner was the fire kindled, than all the people set up a great shout. It was impossible to have heard the woman had she groaned or even cried aloud on account of the mad noise of the people, and it was impossible for her to stir or struggle on account of the bamboo poles which held her down like the levers of a press. We could not bear to see more."

The angry Carey went into action. He collected evidence showing that in one six-month period, around Calcutta alone, nearly 300 widows had been burned—10,000 in all of India. Carey bombarded the British government with persistent protests until the government, by a specific regulation on December 4, 1812, forever forbade these terrible murders by burning.

So also Carey arose in wrath when he saw mothers hurling their babies into the waters of the sacred Ganges River to drown. Female babies were also killed by their mothers, if it was thought unlikely that they would get husbands in their own caste.

Once more Carey, vigorously protesting, moved the government to put a stop to these unhuman practices. There seemed to be no end to the horrors he had to fight. Appalled at the sight of lepers being burned alive, he promoted the founding of a lepers' hospital in Calcutta.

By now, he well understood that in preaching the gospel, a missionary had to work against every form of evil and injustice. His work required infinite patience, for he labored long years in order to win his first convert. Just as Adoniram Judson was to do later, so Carey worked seven years to win his first disciple to Christ.

It happened rather strangely and quickly. A Hindu, Krishna Pal, fell in some slippery mud on the river bank and suffered excruciating pain from a dislocated shoulder. He was brought to the mission by Carey for relief from his pain. The gospel was preached to him and three days before Christmas, 1800, he confessed Christ, broke bread, and joined with Carey in prayer.

A mob of 2,000 surrounded Krishna Pal's home, cursing, threatening, and finally dragging him to the judge who ordered him imprisoned. Carey secured his release. As his baptismal day drew near, kin and neighbors renewed their taunts and threats against Krishna Pal. But, on December 28, 1800, just seven years after Carey had reached India, he had the unspeakable joy of leading his first convert into the waters of the river Hugli to be baptized.

It was only one baptism, but an entire continent was to follow after him. In fact, before very long, Carey had the joy of counting more than a thousand baptized.

One day a ship just arrived from England brought great good news to Carey in a letter from a young printer and editor by the name of William Ward. The magnetism of Carey's ambitious purpose had attracted Ward. "I'm coming to visit you," the letter said. "You once told me you would need someone to print the Scriptures — it is in my heart to live and die with you, to spend and be spent with you."

Carey was overjoyed at the arrival of this energetic printer, who proved to be the strong right arm of his mission.

Great plans were immediately made for printing the gospel by the hundreds. But where could the paper be obtained? The native rice paper was impractical, for white ants devoured it. The man who had made shoes was not to be stumped. Soon, with Ward's help, he was operating the first paper mill — and for forty years the only paper mill — in India.

Ward was not long in building a first-class printing plant and type foundry.

Assisted by capable and loyal associates like Joshua and Hannah Marshman, Carey worked feverishly to translate the Bible into Bengali. Before the observance of the Lord's Supper one Sunday in 1801, he triumphantly laid on the communion table the first copy of the Bible printed in a native tongue of India. It was an unforgettable day! Perhaps Carey's greatest work and that to which he gave his first devotion was the translation of the Holy Scriptures.

By 1818 the presses were rolling, and portions of the Bible translated under Carey were being printed in forty different languages and dialects. The printing plant turned out one hundred thousand tracts annually. Added to this, Carey created a Bengali dictionary of eighty thousand words.

The printers were on fire with the Holy Spirit. "Unto me who am less than the least of all saints is this grace given, that I should print for the Gentiles the unsearchable riches of Christ," wrote Ward.

Carey's vision and drive animated all his helpers. "I would not exchange my occupation in this Scripture printing office," declared Brundson, another helper, "to be the Archbishop of Canterbury."

The distinguished scholarship of even a humble Baptist missionary could not be hidden. An honorary degree was conferred upon Carey. Just at the time when the mission funds were low and Carey was nearly penniless, the Governor General made him professor of native languages at Calcutta College. The position carried a generous salary, which Dr. Carey poured back into the work of his Serampore Mission. This he continued to do throughout his forty years of labor in India. He led his fellow missionaries to turn back their earnings too into a common brotherhood fund.

Out of this voluntary sharing in common, the mission workers founded and erected in 1821 Serampore College. The man whose formal education had begun and ended in the Paulerspury village school had founded the first Christian college in all of Asia. The beautiful Greek structure with its impressive columns was a monument expressive of the educational and spiritual objectives of the mission.

Dr. Carey's plan of self-support was so successful that at the end of his forty years' labor, he had earned and contributed to the work of the mission the sum of about $46,-625. In all that time, the Baptist Missionary Society in Britain, which he had founded, had given him only $600 for the support of himself and family.

This was exactly as Carey would have had it. The mission came first, always. His secular interests were secondary.

In 1812, Adoniram and Ann Hasseltine Judson stayed with Dr. Carey on their first arrival in India. Ann was enthralled with the two-acre garden which was Carey's special botanical hobby. She declared it was more beautiful than anything she had ever seen in America. As they walked and

61

talked in the garden, the Judsons perhaps reminded Dr. Carey that his example had not only inspired them and thousands of Baptists in America, but that it had also led to the founding of the Church of England Missionary Society in 1795, the London Missionary Society in 1795, and the British and Foreign Bible Society in 1804. Carey was too modest to tell them that he would be founding also the first Botanical Society in India. Instead, he spoke of the numerous mission stations in India, Burma, and China which he had begun, the plans he envisioned for extending the work, and his hope that they would accept the challenge of Burma.

Still a young woman in a foreign land, Ann was eager with questions. "Dr. Carey, is it true that three attempts have been made to murder you?"

"Yes," he replied tersely.

"Is it true that a few years ago the government forbade you and your missionaries to preach or distribute tracts or send out native preachers?"

"Yes," Carey smiled, "but at midnight I aroused Henry Martyn and together we took hold of the horns on the altar in fervent prayer and somehow we knew that our foes would be foiled."

"Oh, and besides," sympathized Ann, "there was this terrible fire and the five deaths in your mission family in less than three months."

"Yes," reflected Dr. Carey, "that fire came in the midst of our mourning and was so fierce that nothing could survive the furnace of flames. Our printing house, plates, type, paper, most of our manuscripts and translations — the building — all were gone."

In a hushed voice Ann asked him, "How did you get the courage to rebuild immediately, and how do you carry on so undauntedly?"

"Oh, it was not through courage of mine," said Carey, "but through the grace of God. Let me show you my path of strength." He led the Judsons along a path in his walled garden to a lovely bower. "This is my sanctuary of prayer and meditation. Here at sunrise, usually about five o'clock, I come to pray aloud, talking to God among these flowers which I so dearly love and which speak to me of the beauty and the power of God. Here I feel the fragrance and loveliness of my Lord and Master. I leave the garden at six o'clock for breakfast and work. Before tea and after supper (when the moon restrains the snakes) I come again for brief prayer, with the Bible in my hand for meditation."

The memory of this garden conversation must have often refreshed the Judsons amid their Burma hardships later.

As for William Carey, he was yet to experience tragedy more devastating by far than the fire which had destroyed his printing plant, the cyclone which had shattered his beautiful garden, the flood which had swept away his home, the financial depression which had caused the loss of all the invested funds of his mission, the insanity and death of his first wife, and the death of his second wife also. All these trials Carey endured, sustained by the grace of God.

But he was hurt to the quick by the false and malicious charges which were directed against him by his Baptist brethren in Britain. The great leaders who had supported his early enterprise, Fuller, Ryland, Sutcliff, and others were dead. Now a new and younger generation had come into leadership of the Missionary Society of England. They were men who did not know Carey personally, and some of them apparently were moved by cocky irresponsibility. One of the English Baptist leaders even vowed to destroy Carey and his mission.

False brethren stabbed William Carey with his deepest wounds. Although he was able to clear himself of all false charges in the minds of all reasonable men, nevertheless, this dedicated man went through the "refiner's fire" to the very last, wounded "in the house of his friends."

Dr. William Carey, cobbler, pastor, linguist, missionary, scholar, builder, translator, great adventurer for Christ, never returned to his native land of England. He never saw again the fields he had roamed as a lad, the churches he had served as pastor, or the friends and family he had left behind him forty years before. Yet he still loved England, for his joy was unbounded when he planted seeds that were sent to him in a box of English soil. His delight became rapture when

63

out of the soil there bloomed a few English daisies. These had been his favorite flower in the meadows of Paulerspury, and he had kept them on the windowsill in his cobbler shop at Moulton.

He wrote to thank his friend for the daisy seeds: "That I might be sure not to lose any part of your valuable present, I shook the bag over a patch of earth in a shady place. On visiting the spot a few days afterwards, to my inexpressible delight, I found a *bellis perennis* of our English pastures springing up. I do not know that I ever enjoyed, since leaving Europe, a simple pleasure so exquisite as the sight of this English daisy afforded me, not having seen one for thirty years and never expecting to see one again."

The wear and tear of the years of hardship and disappointment at last weakened the body of this man. The time came when he could only enter his beloved garden in a wheelchair.

One June night in 1834, he slept very deeply and, about the time of sunrise, his favorite hour of prayer, he laid down his earthly burdens in the silence of a radiant morning.

The friends who wept around his bier could not hear the bells of heaven ringing to welcome a valiant pilgrim home to heaven, but they knew that their great friend could announce to the Master, "Mission accomplished."

He had, indeed, expected great things from God and, therefore, he had achieved great things for God. He was born a common man, but he had fulfilled his determination to become an uncommon man in the service of his God.

CHAPTER 7

ADONIRAM JUDSON

The Pioneer American Missionary

WITH A LEAP, the young man mounted his horse, spurred the beast to a swift gallop, and headed west out of New York state, he scarcely knew why.

His brain still reeled from the shock he had received early that morning. "Anywhere," he thought; "anywhere to get away and to clear my agonized mind."

Suddenly, though, he drew tight rein and stopped his horse. "Going west will not answer," he told himself. "My problem is too desperate."

Quickly he turned his mount around, and galloped hard toward his father's home. Sparks flew from his horse's well-shod hoofs as he urged him over the narrow New England roads toward Plymouth, Mass., on that frosty morning in late September, 1808. This young man had no eyes for the lush autumn foliage of scarlet and yellow which festooned the highway, for his mind was absorbed with the tragedy of the past night in the country inn where he had lodged.

How jauntily he had accepted the innkeeper's apology when he candlelighted him up the narrow stairs to his room. "We are full up, young sir, and this is the only room left. There is a very sick man in the next room, in fact he may even be dying, but I believe you will not be disturbed."

"Don't worry," said the gay youth just turned twenty. "I have just quit a shabby theatrical troupe and got out of New York City. I'm so dog tired from the long journey that I'll sleep as sound as a log tonight." "Besides," he added to him-

65

self, "I'm no longer burdened with my father's simple concerns about salvation and heaven. I'm an intellectual, facing life stoically as an infidel should. Yes, I shall sleep."

Young Adoniram Judson blew out the candle in his bedroom and fell into bed. But somehow the dark had an eerie quality. "Dying," did the innkeeper say? "Oh, well it's no skin off my nose."

Furthermore, there were creaking boards, hushed voices, and deep groans behind the thin partition. Somehow the angel of sleep did not help young Judson that night.

Near the wee morning hours, the weird noises ceased. There was only the silence and the deep darkness. At long last he dozed.

When he awoke, the sun was up throwing shafts of light across his bed and face. Blue jays were cawing sharp warnings in the wood. The robins were cheerlessly singing for rain. From the inn kitchen the aroma of fried eggs and ham filtered into his room. Adoniram jumped out of bed and hurriedly dressed for breakfast.

Downstairs in the dinning room, the innkeeper looked haggard. "I had a hard night," he complained to Judson. "That young man in the room next to yours died."

"Oh, a young man was he?" Judson was surprised. Like most young people, he had assumed that death was something that happens only to the aged.

"Yes," said the innkeeper. "It's very sad. He seemed to be such a nice young fellow. He was — let me see — oh yes, a fellow from Brown University over in Providence. His name, I believe, was Jacob Eames."

Instantly, Judson sprang up. His face close to the innkeeper's, he exclaimed incredulously, "Did you not say Jacob Eames? No! Not Jacob Eames!"

"That's the name, young sir," said the innkeeper.

Judson fell back limp into his chair. "My God," he cried, "my college classmate and my best friend, dying in the next room while I slept! Eames! Why, he was an agnostic. He may be lost." Suddenly Judson put his head down on the table and wept. Afterward, for a long time, he sat staring at the table, too shaken to eat.

Presently he rose and left the inn, and with some thought of escaping his grief he began the westward journey. His infidel beliefs had failed him in the time of crisis.

Judson had not ridden far when the desolation of his unbelief overwhelmed him. Suddenly he longed for the sustaining comfort of his father's faith and it was for this reason that he turned back. After a hard week's ride, he arrived at his father's house, broken and exhausted.

But once returned to the fireplace in the parsonage of the Plymouth Congregational Church, he felt again the healing warmth of his mother's love and of his father's faith. In the days that followed, he spent many long hours in the study with his father. Their earnest discussions bore fruit in Adoniram's changed outlook. They established in him a firm Christian belief. A few weeks later he joined a group of fervent Christian students who were enrolling in Andover Theological Seminary, located a few miles from Boston.

But at twenty there are more subjects than theology on an active young man's mind, as Adoniram was soon to discover.

Along with some other ministers attending the association meeting, he was invited to dinner at Deacon Hasseltine's home in Bradford, a town not far from the seminary. The deacon's daughters, Ann, Abigail, and Mary, had been bustling about with their mother all day roasting turkey, cooking cranberry sauce, plum pudding, apple pies, and hot cinnamon rolls.

Ann, paring apples, grew dreamy. "I wonder what that young Judson they talk so much about will be like."

"Well, at least you know he's brilliant," Mary told her. "He was valedictorian of his class in college and they say he's the leading scholar in his class at the seminary."

"Yes, yes, but I wonder what he looks like," persisted Ann. "Is he tall?"

"No," said her younger sister flatly. "I passed him face to face on the campus last week. He's a small man and I think his nose is a bit long."

"But," Ann argued, "isn't that supposed to be a sign of a positive personality?"

Mary laughed. "His eyes are as sharp as a chipmunk's, and a sparkling, beautiful brown, if you must worry about him."

"Worry?" Ann shrugged. "Why should I worry? I never intend to get married."

As he sat down to the dinner table in the Hasseltine home that day, Adoniram saw her first. His eager eyes drank in the beauty of her olive skin framed with raven locks and of her luminous eyes, reflecting light like dark pools. How dainty, how gracious, how beautiful she was!

Ann, waiting on the table, reached over his shoulder to place his dinner plate in front of him. Her arm brushed his shoulder sending delicious quivers through his body. "What perfume does she wear?" he wondered. "It smells like the April arbutus."

Ann eyed him cautiously while she cut the pie at a side table. "He talks of going to foreign countries to preach the gospel," she reflected. "He must be ambitious and adventurous. And no matter what Mary says, I like his high forehead and intelligent face. But he doesn't even bother to look at me. He must be the bachelor type or an egotist."

How could she know that already he was so paralyzed by love of her that he wasn't able to look up? He could only stare at the linen tablecloth, while composing in his mind a love poem to Ann's beauty.

When Papa Hasseltine shook hands with Judson that night, he said: "Young man, your idea of preaching the gospel to those faraway foreigners sounds very radical to me. In this fast-growing country, there is lots of work to be done for God. A young man with your brilliant mind can get a big pulpit in a city church. No need, Judson, to throw yourself away over there in India. Think it over. Good night."

Unmoved by this temptation to stay safely at home while serving a nice American church, Judson relentlessly pursued his purpose to attempt personally the adventure of a mission to the heathen. His zealous dedication to Christ and the positive force of his challenge to his elders finally won them over to his ideas. Other seminary students joined him in demanding that Christians wake up to their duty to preach the gospel to the heathen in foreign lands. As a result, the first overseas mission from America to the distant heathen was organized in Massachusetts in the summer of 1810.

All set to go now, Judson turned his eyes and heart upon beautiful Ann Hasseltine. He needed her for his companion and wife to share his great adventure and its perils. Would she go with him? There could be no doubt there, for sweet Christian girl that she was, she had written him on New Year's day: "With my whole heart, my love, I wish you a happy New Year. . . . May this be the year in which you will take final leave of your native land and cross the wide ocean and dwell on the other side of the world, among a heathen people."

Yes, Ann would follow him to the ends of the earth amid all the perils. But what of her father, stern old Deacon Hasseltine? Would he consent? Judson faced that problem when he carefully penned a letter to him asking Ann's hand in marriage.

Deacon Hasseltine was standing by the front window when he opened the letter. As he read, his face reddened to the roots of his hair. "Sir, can you consent to part with your daughter early next spring, to see her no more in this world?" The deacon's hand gripped the back of a chair to steady himself from the blow which hit him hard upon the heart. "Can you consent to her departure to a heathen land and her subjection to hardships and sufferings of a missionary life . . . to degradation, insult, persecution, and perhaps a violent death?"

The letter shook in Deacon Hasseltine's hand, which now was all atremble. This young man came to his point with a stunning force. There was no attempt at deception or cleverness. Yet the letter ended with an appeal which overcame the good deacon's opposition. "Can you consent to all this for the sake of Him who left His heavenly home and died for her and for you?"

Alarmed as the father was, even he could not foresee that all the hardships which Judson predicted for Ann would indeed come true in far, faraway Burma.

Now that he had won Ann securely, there remained one
more barrier — one further temptation. His own father and
mother, who had sacrificed, prayed, and dreamed for his future, now pleaded with him to give up his rash mission to
the heathen and preach the gospel in nearby Boston. His
college wanted him to teach, and the leading pulpit of Boston was trying to secure his services. The prospects for success at home were flattering; the prospects for success with
the heathen were slim indeed.

"Can't you see we need you here in our old age to inspire
and cheer us?" his parents begged.

"The Lord calls me to go," said Judson as he embraced
them. "I hear the trumpets calling. I cannot stay longer.
Good-bye. I leave you in the care of our heavenly Father."

Once more he mounted his horse, but this time it was to
meet Ann whom he just married. After his ordination they
bade friends, home, and country farewell, and sailed from
Salem harbor on the brig "Caravan" outbound for Calcutta,
India. It was just a week before Valentine's Day, February
7, 1812. Judson was a young man in a hurry, for in three
days he had married, had been ordained, and had sailed
away.

Even the War of 1812, fought largely by sea between the
United States and Great Britain, did not deter Judson from
his firm purpose. Neither did the stiff wintry wind that was
blowing up a storm, nor the black clouds banked along the
far horizon. Nor was Judson afraid of his country's enemies
and their fighting ships. He had seen too clearly the providence of God guiding his steps to be fearful of the sea, the
storm, or the blood of battle.

As the brig fought her way around the Cape of Good
Hope, Ann asked him, "How much longer will it be before
we arrive in India?"

"We should reach Calcutta by the end of the first week of
June," Adoniram answered hopefully.

Ann tried hard to be cheerful also. "One hundred and
twenty days shut up in this little ship is long enough."

"It has been hard for you, Ann, I know, but think what
a blessing it has been to have had all this time to study our

Bible together! This enforced seclusion has led us to our mission in a new light. According to the New Testament, belief in Christ must come first, and then comes the ordinance of baptism. If we are to start a new colony of Christians, I'm now sure that it must be of the Baptist faith, for the Baptists are right according to the Scriptures."

"I agree with you," said Ann. "But the Congregationalists ordained you and sent you out here in good faith. How can you now decide that they are wrong and desert them to become a Baptist?"

Judson thrust his hands into his trouser pockets, lowered his head, and walked down the deck away from Ann. His brow was drawn in anxious meditation. Here, indeed, was a grave problem. Should he keep quiet about being a Baptist and just go on working as if he were still a Congregationalist? Always there were these tough problems bobbing up unexpectedly, always these new temptations to make some compromise.

But young Judson was too honest and straightforward for any double dealing. He preferred to take the risk of being stranded on a foreign shore without support from home and without portfolio except the command of Christ.

A letter written by Ann best recounts their distress: "But because we are compelled to be, we have endeavored to count the cost and be prepared for the many severe trials resulting from this change of sentiment.

"We anticipate loss of reputation and of the affection and esteem of our American friends. . . . These things have caused us to weep and pour out our hearts in prayer to Him whose directions we so much wish and need.

"We feel that we are alone in the world with no real friend but each other, no one on whom we can depend but God."

On landing in India, he and Ann forthwith were baptized in Calcutta on September 6, 1812. Coming up out of the water Judson kissed Ann saying, "My dear, you are the first American woman ever to go as a foreign missionary to the heathen, and now we both are the first missionaries whom the Baptists of America have ever had among the heathen." 71

Their faces were radiant as they knelt side by side in prayer and lifted up their hearts toward God.

While in India they visited the famous missionary, William Carey, who advised them to go to Rangoon, Burma, and open a mission there. Rangoon was a place where the need was great and where only strong pioneers could endure. On Thursday, July 2, 1813, the Burmese beheld two foreigners landing in their city. They were sick and weak from a rough voyage that had taken them many days, and during which death had almost claimed them. Ann had to be carried into Rangoon, for at that time she was too weak to walk.

It was a full sixteen months after they left Salem, Mass., that their mission was begun. They were in a land of eight million brown-skinned people of subject races and half-wild tribes scattered in dirty villages through the jungles. The people were worshipers of Buddha or were animists, and they showed no sign of wanting a new religion. There was no welcome for the Judsons.

Besides the indifference of the people, there was the danger of snakes, scorpions, elephants, wild cats, centipedes, cobras, leopards, and tigers. Moreover, it was an unruly land where life was cruel and unsafe and anything might happen. The dirt, unhealthy food, and unsanitary conditions made the danger of disease a constant threat.

Though at first they were lonely, isolated, and depressed, the Judsons were immensely cheered a few months later by word that the Baptist people of America had taken them to their hearts and were sending money for their support. In fact, the news of the Judsons as new Baptist missionaries had electrified the scattered Baptists of the United States, thanks to the vigorous crusade of their friend, Luther Rice.

Almost overnight the Baptists were stirred by the eloquent appeals of this friend of the Judsons to organize missionary societies. Inspired by the example of the Judsons, the Baptists sent delegates who met in Philadelphia and who, on May 18, 1814, organized a missionary crusade which they called by the tedious name, "The General Missionary Convention of the Baptist Denomination in the United States for Foreign Missions."

Judson found that winning his first convert to Christ in the land of Burma was a slow work and one that required patient endurance. On the highway to the Shwe Dagon, the golden pagoda which was the pride of Rangoon's ten thousand people, Judson had built a curious gospel hut as a means of reaching the passers-by. It was a thatched-roof shanty, twenty by thirty feet in size, called a *zayat*. In front was a ten-foot porch where Judson would sit and invite tired travelers to rest awhile. There, engaging them in religious conversation, he would tell them about the one true God and his Son, Jesus Christ.

Among the Burmese who came and listened and went away and later came again and again, was a man named Maung Nau, who worked for a teakwood merchant. After listening to Judson for more than six years, Maung Nau one May day "declared himself a disciple of Christ in the presence of a considerable number of people." Here at long last was Judson's first convert — or was he?

He *was*, for a few days later Maung Nau wrote Judson a beautiful letter asking baptism. "It is through the grace of Jesus Christ," Judson read, "that you, sir, have come by ship from one country and continent to another and that we have met together. I pray my Lord that a suitable day may be appointed and that I may receive the ordinance of baptism."

On Sunday, June 27, 1819, just seven years and four months after his departure from the United States, Judson baptized Maung Nau in a large pond. From the bank, the enormous image of Gautama Buddha bent downward its contemplative gaze upon the company and the immersion.

Soon other converts came, and there in Rangoon Judson organized a little Baptist church of ten members.

The Emperor now threatened to kill anyone who accepted the new religion. Therefore when Moung Ing, the fisherman, wanted to be baptized, Judson warned him that he risked his life. "Do you love Christ better than your own life?" the missionary asked him.

Moung Ing replied very deliberately and solemnly, "When I meditate on this religion, I know not what it is to love life."

Moung Shwe-gnoug also desired to be baptized. "Do you really love Christ?" asked Judson.

With feeling, the old man answered, "No one who really knows him can help loving him."

Of such staunch converts, Judson built the foundations of his mission in Burma.

These first victories, after seven years of effort, had exacted a heavy cost. The Judsons had buried their first son, Roger, in a lonely grave. They had suffered from fever, and had been exposed to cholera and other epidemics; they had endured the mental anguish of war scares and threats of banishment. They had suffered robberies. They had been separated for seven months, during which rumors of Judson's death had tormented Ann beyond description. But worse trials were to follow. There would be imprisonment and the most painful tortures.

The Judsons had moved to a place called Ava, near the Emperor's seat of government. Judson had hoped to intercede with the Emperor to secure liberty for his mission to preach the gospel freely to the people of Burma.

Judson appeared at court with his plea for the right to preach the one true God in that country whose religion taught that there was "no god to save, no soul to be saved, no sin to be saved from." The Emperor rejected Judson's petition in anger. It was a warning of the troubles to come.

At the outbreak of the war between England and Burma, Judson was still in Ava. He had been busy translating into the Burmese language the Gospel of Matthew, the Letter to the Ephesians, and the Book of Acts.

When the British fleet bombarded Rangoon, many foreigners were arrested as spies. The Judsons, too, fell under suspicion. On a Tuesday in June of 1824, just as they were about to sit down to dinner, men pushed open the door and charged into their little home.

Ann froze with horror at sight of the lead man, Spotted Face, a repulsive brute with two circles tattooed on his cheeks. He was a well-known criminal and was presently executioner at the prison. So depraved was he that he enjoyed making others suffer the most cruel pain.

Spotted Face hurled himself at Judson, knocking the missionary to the floor. Then he sprang on top of him, digging his knees into his stomach. He drew a hard cord around Judson's arms, tying them in such a position behind him as to cause great pain, sometimes almost stopping his breath. Judson was dragged off to prison, while Ann tried vainly to obtain his release by offering money.

In the prison courtyard his tormentors lifted Judson's feet to a granite block and riveted upon them three pairs of ankle fetters. "Walk now, you teacher!" they taunted him. In trying to take a single step, Judson fell upon his face.

Next he was dragged into a cell without a window. The darkness, stifling hot, reeked with a nauseating stench. By the dim light from a small doorway, Judson could discern some fifty naked prisoners around him.

When night came, a long bamboo pole was slipped between Judson's ankle fetters, and his feet, secured to the pole, were hoisted up toward the ceiling so that only his shoulders and head rested on the floor.

Rats and vermin plagued the prisoners, and Judson's hair and shoulders became smeared with slimy filth. His ankles were raw, chafed by the three heavy iron fetters, and the cord which held his arms in the tortured position caused deep, festering cuts in his flesh. Judson felt death to be very close, about to snatch him — and poor Ann — in its jaws.

After some days Judson was removed to the death house. There he lay on his back with a thirty-two pound weight on his feet, which again were hoisted upward on a bamboo pole. The temperature was 100 degrees and the stench sickening. Talking was forbidden.

Each day at three o'clock a gong sounded and Spotted Face came in and led some prisoner out to his death.

Brave Ann used every art and scheme she could devise in order that she might see her husband. At length, by paying the government $100, she obtained permission to visit him.

As she entered the prison, dread black birds crawled out of the murky darkness toward her. Spotted Face shouted a malevolent, "Get out!" But the gently reared daughter of

Deacon Hasseltine walked courageously into the death house to see her husband.

Somehow she persuaded the governor to allow Judson and Price, his missionary companion, to be moved into an open-sided shed where they could breathe a little fresh air. The few prisoners thus housed were permitted to go to a gate for food. Ann managed to send Adoniram a note, hidden in a bowl of rice, and she provided Judson and Price each with a white pillow.

Eventually husband and wife learned to exchange notes rolled up and placed in the long nose of a teapot — for Ann was allowed to bring hot tea to her husband each day. Later, she was permitted to spend an hour visiting him in the open shed.

Adoniram was greatly worried about the safety of his manuscript of the New Testament which he had translated into the Burmese language. It represented years of patient work. For safekeeping, Ann had buried it in the garden back of their little living place.

Adoniram instructed her to dig up the manuscript. "Put it in an old-looking pillow," he directed. "Make it feel so hard that no jailer would ever want to steal it."

Thus Judson, in his prison, slept on the New Testament he had translated — the only copy of the Burmese New Testament in all the world!

With quiet heroism Ann Judson ministered to her husband, walking each day the two miles to the prison and the two miles returning. She did this for more than seven months. Besides, each day, she visited some officer of the government, presenting her gifts and her entreaties, always seeking to ease the hardships of the prisoners and trying to win deliverance for Adoniram.

Adoniram was in prison eleven months. The birth of their baby interrupted Ann's visits. Soon after her confinement, she was stricken with an all but fatal disease. At this same time, Adoniram was smitten with a terrible fever. Only through the fidelity of their Bengalese cook, who carried food daily to both Adoniram and Ann, were their lives saved.

The war between Burma and Britain now ended, and with

its ending, Judson was released from prison. Once more, brave, faithful Ann returned from Ava to Rangoon, side by side with her husband.

Then came what was for Judson the hardest blow of all. While he was away on a trip, the news reached him that Ann, in Rangoon, had died. Soon their little child, Maria, died also. Lovely Ann and her two children were in their graves. Judson now was alone in a strange land.

For long months the faith of Adoniram Judson suffered its severest trial. The man was overcome with a deep depression of spirit. Through agonizing weeks he searched prayerfully for the true meaning of his mission and the will of God for him. At last, after many months, he took fresh courage. A spirit of triumph was granted to him by Christ. He arose once more to take up his work with new zest and with an abiding confidence.

Judson continued to serve in Burma for many years, preaching, baptizing, translating, building schools, and new mission stations. By the year 1834, he had completed the translation of the entire Bible into Burmese. When this laborious work was completed, he fell on his knees and, holding the last page of the translation in his hand, he prayed God to "make his own inspired word, now complete in the Burmese tongue, the great instrument of filling all Burma with songs of praise to our great God and Savior, Jesus Christ."

Soon after this he baptized his one hundredth Karen convert and also his one hundredth Burmese convert. He presided over a mission which now numbered one thousand converted Christians.

It would take much too long to recount in any detail the remaining years of Judson's life. The story of his later marriages and of his work on the English-Burmese dictionary must be left to other books.

When, in 1845, Judson visited America after an absence of thirty-three years, those who came to welcome this valorous soldier of the cross did not see the young man of robust health to whom they had bidden farewell when he sailed from Salem in 1812. Instead, they greeted a frail man whose

health had been broken by malignant malaria and privations, whose body bore the scars caused by cruel fetters, whose voice was so weak that it could scarcely be heard in a public address. Yet his presence as an honored Christian pioneer and courageous fighter for Christ everywhere enheartened those who saw and heard him.

Judson returned to Burma, but his health was too precarious to sustain him long in his labors. His doctors advised a long sea voyage, and he died on shipboard, April 12, 1850. That same day, his body was lowered into the sea which received in silence the mortal frame of his immortal spirit.

The influence of this dauntless warrior of Christ abides powerfully not only in Burma but also among all Baptists. Furthermore his life is an inspiration wherever Christians, regardless of their denominations, are moved by the Great Commission: "Go ye into all the world, and preach the gospel to every creature."

CHAPTER 8

LUTHER RICE

Pioneer Promoter and Organizing Genius

"THEY'RE GETTIN' UP a lumberin' party to go down to Georgia to cut some of the tall timber for these here new square-rigger sailin' ships they're a-buildin' in New Bedford and Boston," announced one of the farmers leaning on the counter in the general store in Northboro, Mass.

An older tiller of the soil deftly snatched up a piece of molasses candy when the storekeeper was not looking and joined in the conversation. "Yeah, they've cut off our best lumber here in New England, so we've got to go to t'other end of the world, way down in Georgia, to git somethin' to build our ships with."

"That'll be one big doin'," observed the Yankee store-keeper. "If I was a mite younger, I'd up and join the party, by jumpin' Jupiter! I'd like to sail down the coast again, like when I was in the Navy."

It was the year 1799, a decade or more after the Revolutionary War had ended and a dozen years before the War of 1812 was to begin. The young nation was feeling a power-ful surge of pioneering energy, and the building of trading ships to sail the high seas was a flourishing business.

The sixteen-year-old boy who had been listening intently to this bit of news now casually inquired, "When is this lumberin' party leavin' for Georgia?"

"I hear," the storekeeper told him, "that, come high tide, they're a-sailin' out o' Boston on Tuesday."

80   The next morning young Luther Rice did not appear at

the family breakfast table. His frantic father and mother inquired about his whereabouts, and it was the storekeeper who offered the clue.

"I thought I spied a look o' romancin' adventure in that lad's eyes when we fell to discussin' the Georgia lumberin' party. I reckon you'll find him with an axe in his hands, a-choppin' tall trees deep in the forest in Georgia."

Luther Rice was always to be a lover of ocean voyages, of distant places, of tough challenges, and of big adventures. The boldness and daring of the runaway boy revealed the characteristics which would distinguish him as a man, and make him one of the greatest pioneer promoters and organizers the Baptists ever had.

His early trip south helped him, throughout his life, to see South and North as one, and prepared him to be at home wherever there was work to be done for God, whether in India or Washington, Carolina or New England.

He was not yet a Christian, but he was a youth who dared to look at himself honestly. He wrote in his journal, "My heart is often, if not constantly filled with impure lust, unholy affection and many of the most odious and detestable pollutions." He longed for a life clean as a sheet of fresh, white paper.

His spiritual struggle lasted from his seventeenth to his nineteenth year. He tested the meaning of decision for Christ in a unique way. He questioned himself thus: "Would I be willing to place a blank sheet of paper with my name at the foot of it in the hand of God, asking him to write upon it my destiny, as it might seem good in his sight?"

When he could answer yes to this, he wrote: "I then found in this position of absolute unreserved submission to the Word of God, a sweet and blessed tranquility. I had become reconciled to God." It was a straightforward, full surrender. In his own fine words, he was "absolutely at the disposal of God." This, of course, is the kind of person God always can use best to get his work done in the world.

He became a devout member of the Congregational church, and his youthful zeal in holding prayer meetings and in trying to convert those who were not Christians stirred 81 up some opposition in the town. Even his father opposed his religious enthusiasm. People said that religion made the boy "mentally unbalanced."

Eventually his father's opposition drove Luther from his home, where he had planned to remain as a farmer. Later, he saw this as the providence of God.

About this time he probably suffered unrequited love. "I sat up late reading a book . . . *Religious Courtship,*" he wrote in his journal. "Perhaps I should suffer less in the singing school if I did not see Miss ———— there. I love her or rather have a passionate propensity toward her. But this passion I must resist — unless I see a real change in her. Oh, what a pitiful case I am in!"

But it was another girl who won his deepest affection. "Ever since I first heard of her, I have desired to get acquainted with her in hope that at some future time she will become my bride."

Later, he wrote, "I went this day to Worcester, principally from a desire of seeing her. The Lord granted my desire."

Another day, after a thunderstorm, he wrote in his diary, "I dreamed considerable about her whom I desire for my wife."

This unknown miss, however, never became his bride. Luther Rice remained a lifelong bachelor, though his journal showed him to have been a man capable of romantic thoughts.

Fired with a desire to preach the gospel, he was determined to get a good education. He studied at Leicester Academy, and in the fall of 1807 he entered Williams College in the sophomore class. He taught school at intervals to defray his expenses.

Rice carried his enthusiasm for the work of Christ into his college career. With several other young men, he felt a call to preach the gospel to the heathen. A group of them, when holding a prayer meeting, were caught in a sudden shower, and they took refuge under a haystack on the college campus. This spot has been known since that date as "the birthplace of American Foreign Missions."

82

As a student at Andover Theological Seminary, Rice became a warm friend of Adoniram Judson and his bride-to-be, Ann Hasseltine. Expecting to join the Judsons in their foreign missionary work, he sailed from Philadelphia and reached Calcutta six weeks behind the Judsons.

There, Rice, a staunch Congregationalist, was not a little amazed to witness the baptism of the Judsons. He listened with rapt attention to the sermon Judson preached from Matthew 28:19: "Go ye therefore, and teach all nations, baptizing them. . . ." He was at first deeply disturbed, but as he studied the Scriptures he came to accept another point of view. A few weeks later, he too was baptized — now a convinced Baptist.

Following this sudden change of denomination, it became necessary to secure support from the Baptists into whose fold the Judsons and Rice had now so unexpectedly come. Also, matters must be explained to the Congregationalists who, after all, had sent them out. It seemed wise, therefore, for Rice to return to America.

The ship on which he secured passage slipped through the searching British warships, and finally, in September, 1813, reached New York. After visiting Baptist friends of the Judsons in Boston, he went to the Southland on a drive to rally Baptists to support the work of the Judsons, and to unite the weak Baptist churches behind this new foreign missionary adventure.

He was a magnetic figure, tall, erect, and robust. As a speaker he was dramatic in his manner, eloquent in his oratory, and impressive and felicitous in his expression.

Being a bachelor, Rice was free to become an itinerant preacher. Like a sewing needle, he threaded his way among the widely separated Baptist churches, and with strong and purposeful ties he bound them together in their first great common enterprise.

While he was riding the stagecoach between Richmond and Petersburg, a plan of organization flashed into his mind. In May of 1814, he called for a rally of key men in Philadelphia. Only thirty-three men responded, but they represented the leadership among the Baptist churches.

Under Rice's guidance, this group organized the Baptists
for the purpose of promoting world-wide missions. They
chose for their organization a cumbersome name, "General
Convention of the Baptist Denomination in the United
States for Foreign Missions," but they made a wise decision
when they put Luther Rice at the head of it as its working
agent and promotional executive.

Rice was now free to express his love of travel, his warmth
of friendship, and his talent for inspiring men to organize
support behind great causes. His vision and enthusiasm
swept all before him. He covered the length and breadth of
the country in pursuing his mission, sometimes on horseback, sometimes in a two-wheeled gig, and always over the
bad roads of that day.

The countryside through which Rice traveled was mostly
wilderness with scattered clearings for farms and villages.
Going from house to house, from church to church, from
county to county, and from state to state, he collected small
sums of money for foreign missions. Everywhere he enthralled the families he visited with the story of Carey and
the Judsons.

Sometimes Rice got lost on the road, as he once wrote:
"Being obliged to ride in the night, on Friday night I got
lost. The roads in this portion of our country are none of
them fenced, and are mostly through woods. I had to go that
night by roads but little traveled — missed the way, got out
of the roads, at length into mere paths, and ultimately lost
the path — found myself alone in a dreary wilderness, unable
to discover the point of compass; totally ignorant which way
to direct my course, or to find any habitation of men."

In our jet age his rate of travel seems ridiculously, even
incredibly, slow. Yet despite the great difficulties, Rice was
able to report that in a little more than ten months he had
"traveled 6,600 miles in populous and in dreary portions of
the country, through wilderness and over rivers, across
mountains and valleys, in heat and cold, by day and night,
in weariness, painfulness, fastings, and loneliness."

As he traveled, visiting homes and preaching in churches,
something rewarding always happened. Sometimes the con-

tagion of his warmly dedicated spirit roused young men to enter the ministry. Two notable leaders who were his spiritual sons were John Mason Peck, pioneer of American Baptist home missions, and Francis Wayland, preacher and educator.

Similarly, Rice's passion for missions often inspired young men to offer themselves for the mission field. He gathered around him a brilliant galaxy of future Baptist leaders. Included among them was Noah Davis, the first secretary of the American Baptist Publication Society.

His eagerness to help young men led him, with the assistance of Dr. William Staughton, to open a small theological school in Philadelphia. This school grew, and in January, 1822, it was moved to Washington, D. C., where it was established as Columbian College. The founding and maintaining of this college engaged a large portion of Rice's time.

Obviously, he was carrying too many heavy burdens alone. His vision and his enthusiasm often outran the support provided by the Baptist churches. He suffered the usual criticisms that are heaped upon men who dare to adventure.

Columbian College got into financial difficulties, and his critics then began to heap calumny upon him by implying that his financial accounts were faulty. Like many another enthusiast, Rice lacked solid business judgment and thereby left himself open to misunderstanding. As an arouser of fiery emotions where great issues were concerned, he could be careless of small details.

These loomed now as all-important, and the college which Rice had had the vision and courage to establish fell away from Baptist control. Today it is that great institution in the capital known as George Washington University.

Under the shadow of misunderstanding, Rice voluntarily withdrew from further official connection with the Convention which owed its being, chiefly, to him. He also severed his relations with the college which he had founded. His counsel was no longer sought by the leaders. Thus, this lonely bachelor and itinerant preacher, being poor and without salary, was left to drift from home to home and from

85

church to church among his hospitable friends in the Southland, who never deserted him.

Yet Luther Rice was great even in his failure. He spent
most of his declining years as an ill man, going about in his
two-wheeled vehicle drawn by his faithful horse, and bring-
ing inspiration and hope to many an isolated Baptist and to
many a lonely church.

Meanwhile, he maintained a heavy correspondence, writing late into the night. Often he posted as many as twenty
letters a day.

In the last years of his life, he returned to his native New
England on a preaching tour. There, in Providence, R. I.,
in 1832, he suffered a slight stroke of paralysis. Though in
a weakened condition, he continued to preach until September of 1836 when his chronic illness finally claimed his life.

Besides those sorrows which we have related, still another
marked Luther Rice's life. He never was able to return to
Burma to work with the Judsons, as he and they had
planned. He became so deeply involved in America with
missionary organization and with Columbian College that
the time never came for him to return. Perhaps things would
have been different if he had found a wife who would have
been willing to go to Burma with him.

Besides, there is something in the earnestness of Ann Judson's letter to him, which to the imaginative, may possibly
hint some other obscure reason for his failure to return. But
certainly his support of the Judsons was a beautiful devotion.

Rice had given up sailing from Salem with the Judsons
in order that Ann Judson, who would have been the only
woman on the ship, might have a companion in Mrs. Samuel
Newell. Perhaps this was only an impersonal Christian act,
but through it seems to shine the gracious admiration of a
bachelor once disappointed in love.

Mrs. Judson dispatched a number of letters to Luther
Rice, one of which, dated July 5, 1819, is typically beautiful. She wrote:

Dear Brother Rice,

Little did we think at our sorrowful parting . . . that
almost seven years would elapse, and we should be still

writing you. . . . We have ever felt that though the breach which your absence has made in our little family would be filled only by yourself, yet we ought to acquiesce, and quietly submit, if the advancement of the mission made it necessary . . . hence, we have until now patiently submitted to the trial which your long absence has occasioned. But now, my dear Brother Rice, we need missionaries on the ground more than anything beside . . . portions of scripture are to be translated and many other necessary things must be done — but who will do them? Besides, should he [Judson] be sick or die, the work which is now commenced would immediately stop . . . you, my dear brother, are just the person that we need just in this stage of the mission. Your age, judgment, and experience, qualify you in a peculiar manner to be of most essential service in those cases of difficulty and trial, to which we are so frequently subject in this country. . . . Come, oh, come, and reap a harvest of souls from among the Burmans. . . . I will urge two reasons more, and I have done. First, this is a delightful climate . . . secondly, it is a good situation to grow in grace, and prepare for heaven. Come then, dear brother, and spend your last days in using those means for bestowing happiness on others, which are the most directly calculated to advance personal piety, and a preparation for eternal glory. Ever affectionately yours,

NANCY JUDSON

Whatever his personal sorrows and failures, Luther Rice was a great friend and supporter of the Judsons, and but for him they could not have carried on in Burma.

Rice's greatest achievement, however, was his success in getting all the scattered and unorganized Baptist churches finally to unite — one hundred and seventy-five years after the First Baptist Church was established in America — in a mighty movement for missions. To accomplish this with churches as separated and individualistic as the Baptist churches were, was indeed the work of a spiritual genius.

CHAPTER 9

JOHN MASON PECK

Master Builder of the West

"WHO'S THAT A-COMIN'" over the mountain?" asked Abigail Weight, as she looked out of her cabin window in the Berkshires late one August Sunday.

Her husband, Job, rose to peer out. "Looks like that tall, lanky fella who's been a-teachin' school over in Big Hollow Settlement."

"Where's he headin' for this Sunday evenin'? There ain't no school-keepin' on a Sunday. And look, comin' behind him is his wife! And he's sure enough carryin' a baby in his arms!"

"Oh, now I know!" exclaimed Job. "He's the one that's turned Baptist on account of not believin' in havin' his infant baptized. They're on their way to join the Baptist meetin' in the schoolhouse over in New Durham."

"Don't say! My goodness, Job, that's a mite of a walk — seven miles each way over the mountain, and a-carryin' that baby. How're they goin' to stumble that seven miles back, over that windin' rocky path after dark?"

Job settled back in his creaky "rocky chair." "Well, it's good August moonlight tonight, and you know them Baptists are stubborn critters," he observed. "Once they make up their minds, they're tough as ox-hide. Distance ain't no account to them so long as they can hold to their peculiar beliefs."

"What's his name?" Abigail wondered. "Is he the fella they call 'Pick' or 'Peck,' or somethin' like that?"

88

"I heard over in Big Hollow Settlement that his name is John Mason Peck," Job told her. "They say he's a mighty bright fella and a shrewd one too. One of them Connecticut Yankees, born over Litchfield way. By now I'd say he must be 'bout twenty-two years old. Married late—didn't get hitched up until he was twenty."

By that time the stranger and his family had disappeared. Little did Job and Abigail dream that the young farmer-teacher's energetic strides over the mountain were symbolic of the great strides which he would take later as, under commission by the Baptists, he would trek far through forests and over prairies to open up the West to the gospel.

It was indeed his concern for the baby whom he carried to church that August day that had awakened the young father to the Baptist viewpoint. Should they have their newborn infant baptized in the Congregational church? The young Pecks had taken that question seriously to heart. Finally their thorough study of the Bible had convinced them that they should not permit the baptism.

And so it was that, with honest conviction based on Bible reading, they joined the little Baptist church at New Durham, N. Y., in 1811; that is to say, about a year before Adoniram Judson was to sail to Burma as a missionary.

You may be sure that John Mason Peck was not a slow Baptist, for immediately thereafter he wanted to add to his work as a farmer and teacher that of being a preacher. Somewhat cautiously the church recognized his latent talents and licensed him to preach.

Thus, at the age of twenty-two, Peck began a ministry which was to stretch out for forty-six years, and which was to carry him as a pioneer preacher to the West, where he would travel thousands of miles through forests and prairies among the new pioneer settlements. Characteristically, the first sermon he preached was from the text, "Go ye into all the world. . . ." As a man of action, he put this command into practice in a big and personal way, as we shall soon see.

Peck's first church was at Catskill, N. Y., where he remained as pastor for only one year. Since the total annual salary paid him was only $61.95, no one can blame this preacher with a growing family to support for deciding to accept a call to the larger church at Amenia, N. Y. Here he was ordained in 1813. At that time, British and American ships on the Atlantic Ocean and the Great Lakes were fighting the War of 1812.

John Mason Peck had not wholly forsaken his first vocation, nor was he ever to desert it. At Amenia, as at Catskill, he conducted a school while he continued to serve as pastor of the church. Throughout his life, the school and the church were to be his two great motivating concerns.

The earnest devotion of his youth made him ardently dream of serving God in wide fields of great enterprise. "A large part of the American continent . . . is in darkness," he wrote in his diary one night, before he blew out the candle beside his bed. "In the United States there is an abundant field for missionary labor. How I should rejoice if Providence should open a door for my usefulness and labors in this way!"

The ink was scarcely dry upon this entry in his diary, before God started opening the doors and presenting to him a gigantic mission that matched, if it did not surpass, his dreams.

But first some man had to unlock the door, and the one who did so seemed a divinely-sent messenger. When the wild roses were blooming in the valleys and the swallows were swooping in circles over the plowed land, Peck rode horseback to the Warwick Association. There Luther Rice was setting Baptist hearts on fire for foreign missionary work and the support of the Judsons in Burma. Peck listened, and by the preaching of this passionate campaigner for Christ he was stirred as he had never been before.

Luther Rice and John Mason Peck sat down together for a long conversation in Peck's home. The balmy winds of June blew softly through the open windows of the sitting room. Rice recognized Peck's extraordinary abilities at once, and gave him a commission to cover the Baptist churches of Central New York, pleading the cause of missions.

Peck took over his new assignment with almost furious energy. In the first three weeks he traveled four hundred and forty miles on horseback, preached nineteen times, and organized many missionary societies.

But even New York state was not big enough for Peck's dreams. He heard the West calling. In a letter to Luther Rice — a man of action, energy, and enthusiasm like himself — Peck wrote: "Is a permanent mission station in the West being planned? . . . Where would such a mission be located? . . . Would it be best to have schools connected with it? . . . And what education would a man require, to qualify for the job of western missionary?" Peck was trying hard to push wide open the door that Rice had unlocked.

Luther Rice responded warmly. Peck found he must prepare for this pioneer work by getting a better education. Rice wrote him, "You will need a good English education and as much more as possible." Besides this, Rice warned him that he who went West as a missionary must "go West for life."

Peck lost no time. He rushed to Philadelphia and joined four fellow students in the only Baptist school available for training preachers. Dr. William Staughton presided over this school. After the manner of the times, he instructed the young theological students in his own home, directing their reading and tutoring them in certain basic studies.

Here under Dr. Staughton's guidance, Peck drove himself, with sternest discipline, to learn all that he could in a single year. What Peck crowded into that year would leave a modern student aghast. He wrestled with Latin, Greek, and Hebrew, as well as philosophy, theology, and English.

Meanwhile, Peck preached in places in all directions, visited prisons, hospitals, and slums, met Baptist leaders, and laid plans for his great missionary journey to the West. College and seminary — all the schooling that he would ever get — had to be acquired in that one precious year of strenuous study!

Even then, Peck could not be sure that the door would open to let him through to the West. The year of preparation completed, he anxiously awaited the call. The Baptist delegates were gathering in Philadelphia in the first regular meeting of what came to be called the Triennial Convention, and they would decide his future. Fortunately Peck had friends in the leadership of the convention in the persons of Dr. Staughton, his teacher, and Luther Rice, his adviser.

The third and fourth days of the convention brought on the crucial debate. Would the delegates have the vision to accept the challenge or would they turn down Peck's mission to the West? Baptists sometimes did queer things (and still do), and they just might turn him down.

On the third day the convention voted to open a mission in the West, but whom would they decide to send?

On the fourth day the choice fell on Peck and a fellow student, James E. Welch, who was to go with him. All smiles as he left the church, Peck threw his hat into the air for sheer joy. He was vibrant with energy and eager to be on his way.

In impressive services of dedication, the two youths, Peck and Welch, were publicly commissioned by prayer and the laying on of hands to undertake this mission to the West. The services were held in the Sansom Street Baptist Church in Philadelphia, where the capable Dr. Staughton was pastor. He was an Englishman by birth, and had been one of those who had helped to commission William Carey to go to India. Now, he was commissioning two young Americans to go to the West. That night Peck wrote in his diary: "I have now put my hand to the plow. O Lord, may I never turn back — never regret this step. It is my duty to live, to labor, to die as a kind of pioneer in advancing the gospel."

The highest visions take shape and form, sometimes, in a most commonplace fashion. Those neighbors and friends, gathered in Litchfield, Conn., to say farewell, witnessed a most unromantic departure.

Into a one-horse wagon, already piled high with bedding, food, a baby's crib, and a buffalo trunk, John Mason Peck loaded his family. His bonneted wife, with a baby in her arms, sat upon the front seat. Peck climbed up beside her, and slapping the reins over the horse's flanks commanded, "Giddap! Giddap!"

Away they went, the wagon wheels lurching over the rocks in the narrow country road. A cloud of dust soon surrounded them, and the July sun of Litchfield poured its heat upon them. And so was begun the long trek of fifteen hundred miles over poor roads and seldom-traveled trails.

The weary journey extended from July 26, 1817 to December 1, 1817 — a total of one hundred and twenty-five days in the wagon. The hardships of the trip were so severe that when Peck crossed the Mississippi River on the little packet, he was too weak to walk or stand, and had to be carried ashore on a stretcher.

John Mason Peck

An open door? Yes, but what a test of faith! To arrive after weary months, a sick man, dangerously stricken!

A further test awaited Peck and his family. St. Louis then was not anything like the present city. It was a wild and wretched frontier settlement without a school or a church, but crowded with saloons and gambling dens which were frequented by roistering plainsmen, cowboys, freebooters, vagabonds, and ne'er-do-wells. Here everything was so cramped that, sick though he was, Peck, his wife, and children were crowded into a single room.

Yet, the door was open, and despite adversity Peck, assisted by Welch, plunged into his work. They rented the back of a store to serve as a combined school and preaching station. Here Peck began the first Baptist work west of the Mississippi River.

Only two months after Peck's arrival these zealous men held a baptismal service on the shore of that same river, as Peck immersed his first two converts from the new mission. A great crowd stood on the banks, solemnly impressed. Only a few made fun. Without doubt, the door was now widely and permanently opened.

Within three years' time, Peck could count fifty schools (day schools and Sunday schools) that he had established in Illinois and Missouri. When he had arrived there he had found whisky-drinking teachers, illiterate and untrained, in charge of such elementary schools as were then in existence. Wherever possible, he replaced these teachers with sober, well-trained men. He brought together in a society of common fellowship the scattered Baptist churches of these two great states.

93

When Peck discovered that many immigrant families had come West without Bibles, he at once organized the Missouri Bible Society. Through the mud and rain, the snow and ice, he rode horseback, his saddlebags weighted down with Bibles and Christian tracts. He would knock at the door of cabins in the wilderness, and enter with his brisk, warm-hearted greeting. He never left a cabin, however poor, without a gracious prayer and, if possible, without leaving a Bible as a gift.

But the open door which brought him his first successes was to admit a series of disasters.

One of the first of Peck's bitter disappointments came when the academy he had founded at St. Charles, twenty miles from St. Louis, was wrecked by the scandalous life of its headmaster, who proved to be a rogue.

A worse calamity followed in the form of a blow struck by the hand of friends. In 1820 the Baptists who had commissioned Peck as their missionary suddenly deserted him, the convention having decided it could no longer support the work in the West.

When this news reached Peck he was flat on his back, almost in the grip of death — laid low by a sickness brought on by overwork, long travels on horseback, and exposure to all weather and wilderness hazards.

Peck was cut off from his job and left penniless. For a year he was without support and he suffered the loneliness of a rejected missionary. He was unable to understand the narrowness of his fellow Baptists, whose vision was too limited to see the vast needs — and also the great future — of the West.

Did Peck for a moment doubt that God had truly opened the door and called him to his work? If so, his doubts vanished, for new friends arose from among the Massachusetts Baptists, and these came to his rescue. The Massachusetts Baptist Missionary Society agreed to call him as their missionary to the West and to give him the authority of their backing. They did not loosen their purse strings to any great extent, however, for they offered him as a salary only $5.00 a week.

Nevertheless, Peck was so cheered by these evidences of understanding and friendship, that when, in 1826, he was invited back East to visit the churches of New England, he accepted the invitation. For four months he went among these churches, and raised money to establish a theological school in Illinois, where he now lived.

He returned to Illinois and made good his plan to found a seminary. Land for the school was his personal gift of acres from his own farm in Rock Spring, Ill. This Literary and Theological Seminary afterward was moved to Upper Alton, Ill., and became known as Shurtleff College. That college, during its lifetime, sent hundreds of men into the ministry and to the missionary field.

Peck, with his characteristic energy, meanwhile had begun the publication of a weekly religious journal called *The Western Pioneer*. This he edited for many years, in addition to performing his other strenuous labors in connection with founding Sunday schools, missionary societies, and churches. He always kept religious literature in his saddle-bags, for he had a profound belief in the power of the printed word.

New friends rallied to his great missionary enterprise. Dr. Jonathan Going was sent out by the Massachusetts Baptists to advise Peck and give him help. Going and Peck conferred as man to man in great earnestness of spirit as they rode horseback together for three months while they surveyed the fields of need. On the last day of their journey they came to Shelbyville, Ky. There they crowned their friendship and their vision by agreeing on a plan for establishing a national missionary society to be called the American Baptist Home Missionary Society.

Following that, it was not surprising that the American Baptist Publication Society of Philadelphia should turn to Peck for help in its time of need. His dynamic energy and administrative skill were just what the Society needed when, in 1843, it called him to serve as Executive Secretary of its publishing enterprise.

The Society then was at low ebb and in need of a leader able to grapple with complicated problems and to lift the 95

Society out of the doldrums. This Peck did in short order, with characteristic courage, resolution, and vision.

So the young man of Litchfield, Conn., seen coming over the mountain path, his babe in his arms, that August Sunday, became the veteran pioneer of the West, who established Sunday schools, a college and a seminary, founded the American Baptist Home Missionary Society, and rejuvenated the American Baptist Publication Society. He engaged in so many different enterprises that he could be known as "The Man With Twenty Hands."

He was a grand, rough and ready pioneer. His educational work was so significant in the civilizing of the West that Harvard University gave him the honorary degree of Doctor of Divinity.

The old pioneer died at the age of 79, a veteran worn out in his Master's service. Baptists owned in him a master builder of extraordinary vision, enormous energy, and heroic stature. For his singleness of purpose and dedicated energy, God opened unto him "a great door and effectual." He outraced his contemporaries, as if driven by the force of a gale wind. May Baptists be blessed with more of his kind!

CHAPTER 10

WILLIAM KNIBB

Emancipator of Slaves

BILL KNIBB WHISTLED as he worked at the press in the printing shop. The place was Bristol, England; the year was 1822. The morning was young, and so was Bill. He had a job and friends galore, for everybody liked him. His whistling was tuneful and gay, and ceased only when the door opened and two soberly dressed Baptist ministers entered.

Bill greeted the famous men cheerily. "Good morning, Dr. Fuller. Good morning, Dr. Ryland."

"Good morning, William," they responded together.

Something strange in their voices caused the young man to ask anxiously, "Is something the matter? Is something wrong?"

"Yes, Bill." Dr. John Ryland spoke quietly. "We should like to speak to you a moment, alone."

Wonderingly, Bill left the press. Each visitor put an arm lovingly around him. The three walked into the little office and Ryland closed the door.

Fuller began. "Bill, we have news from Jamaica, of your brother, Thomas."

Bill's heart suddenly felt heavy as lead. Three months ago Tom had gone to Jamaica as a missionary to work among the cruelly oppressed slaves of that Caribbean island, and Bill knew that in Jamaica the planters and overseers were vigorously opposed to all Christian missions and sometimes persecuted the ministers.

Painfully, he whispered, "Is Tom in some — trouble?"

97

The men nodded, and Dr. Ryland said, "We have come to
tell you, Bill, that your brother is dead. The news has just
been received. Tom was stricken with fever and could not
recover. He died at his post."

Grief overwhelmed Bill. "Oh, no, no!" he protested. "Not
Tom! Not Tom!" It couldn't be! Tom was so good — so
fine! He and his younger brother had been close companions. Each had taught a Sunday school class in the Baptist
church. They had held meetings together in the slum dis-
tricts of Bristol. They had worked side by side in the Fuller
Printing Shop. They had been so close! "It couldn't be!"
Bill whispered brokenly. He slumped into a chair, buried
his face in his hands, and sobbed.

Nevertheless, Bill heard the minister's words: "A tremendous loss . . . a great grief to us all. . . ." The words didn't
help. Tom had served only four months when he was struck
down.

"Why? Why?" Bill cried. "Tom was doing such a great
work for God! Why would God take him away?"

Fuller laid a gentle hand on the young man's shoulder.
"God's will is sometimes hard to accept, Bill. But in his
time, he will make it plain to you."

At length the young man's weeping quieted. He rose, and
the ministers saw a strange radiance spread slowly over his
tear-stained face. He walked to the window and lifted up
his eyes, and they heard him speak softly, as if to his brother.

"Don't worry, Tom. It's going to be all right. I'm going
to carry on your work for you. Your great work for Christ
is not done — and it shall not stop."

In a moment he turned, looked calmly at the two pastors,
and said, "If the Missionary Society will accept me, I'll go
to Jamaica in Tom's place."

Fuller gazed at him in speechless wonder.

From a full heart, Ryland spoke. "The Missionary Society
will send you, Bill. And God will bless your mission."

Fortunately, the Missionary Society acted swiftly. It agreed
to send William Knibb to Jamaica, there to take the place
of his dead brother, Tom. Bill, accordingly entered upon
three months of intensive training in an institution for

teachers. During that time he married a lovely girl from his church and, in November of 1824, he and his bride set sail for Jamaica.

It is no wonder that this girl had fallen in love with him. He was only twenty-one years of age, and has been described as tall, and popular; and such was his desire for an education that he studied Dr. Johnson's *Dictionary* even at meal times. Clearly, he would be an intelligent and able missionary.

Bill already knew something of the curse of the slavery system which prevailed in all the islands of the West Indies. Moreover, on board the ship when sailing out to his mission field, he was revolted by the conversation of a typical planter and slave owner. In his diary, that night, he recorded his loathing and detestation of the slave trade, using such terms as "odious," "execrable," "infernal," "brutalizing," and "immoral." He declared that slavery called for the "curse of every friend of common decency."

Soon after his arrival at his station in Jamaica he wrote to his mother: "The cursed blast of slavery has, like a pestilence, withered almost every moral bloom. For myself, I feel a burning hatred against it as one of the most odious monsters that ever disgraced the earth."

His heart sank like lead when he first beheld the schoolhouse where his brother had taught. The building was almost a complete wreck.

"We must have a new school and a bigger one," he resolved.

Soon he erected the new school building. It was a day of great joy when he superintended two hundred and fifty Negro children as they marched two by two into their new school.

Bill Knibbs' energy was boundless. Next he built a girls' school close by. He raised the necessary money by letters of appeal to his friends in England.

The day of dedication was colorful. Three hundred pupils in their best attire formed a procession to the school. The dark-skinned girls wore white dresses and carried bouquets of red and purple and yellow flowers. Their curly hair was tied with ribbons of rainbow hues.

As they marched and sang, tears of joy filled Bill's eyes. "Tom," he whispered, "I promised I'd do it in your place."

William Knibb located his brother's chapel in Port Royal, Jamaica, and reopened it with such crowds and overflow of converts that immediately it was necessary to enlarge that building also. As a result of his travels over the island, he drew the scattered Baptists into an organized parish. This parish was established in 1826, and became known as the Jamaica Baptist Association.

William Knibb, though still in his early twenties, and thought to be more teacher than preacher, frequently had a thousand people in attendance at his prayer meetings.

Knibb soon saw, however, that conversions were not enough. He must rid the island of slavery, if he were to preach the gospel in its fulness. Fearlessly he expressed fierce anger against the brutality of the slave owners and declared that slavery should be abolished as indecent and unchristian.

The slaveholding planters, who were enriching themselves by the misery of the slaves, went into prompt action against this young man, whom they considered an intruder.

First, they wanted to know what right Baptists had to meddle with their business. Missionaries had been in Jamaica for a period of years. "Let these missionaries," they said, "make the slaves contented and happy in their gospel meetings, but let them keep their mouths shut about slavery. It is none of their business."

Next the newspapers took up the cry against Knibb.

Finally, the magistrate in Kingston called Knibb to the bench in order to persuade or frighten him to the point of quitting his preaching. Like the first apostle, before the Sanhedrin, Knibb replied, "I am sent here to preach, and preach I must and shall, and I'll take the consequences."

Little did he dream, then, what those consequences would be.

The slaveholders were wickedly determined men and by political maneuvering they got a "commission" appointed to "investigate" the Baptist missionaries and their work. They also published in the newspapers the most vicious lies about Knibb and his fellow Baptist missionaries.

They accused the missionaries of causing sedition and re-
bellion among the slaves and of extorting money from them
by trickery. They even went so far as to charge that the
missionaries encouraged the women to offer themselves for
money, which was turned over to the missionaries.

The slave owners sent thousands of these printed reports
to England, hoping thereby to broadcast these slanders over
the land. Fortunately, the charges were so outrageous and
so obviously untrue that they were not believed by the British people.

"The newspapers teem with unblushing falsehoods against
us," Knibb wrote his friends. "We are called liars, pick-
pockets, vagabonds, scoundrels, and every term of reproach
that malice can invent. If Satan has any shame, I think he
must be ashamed of his agents here."

A typical example of the persecution in Jamaica was that
administered to a converted slave, Sam Sidney. Sam was
a deacon in the Baptist church. Because he offered a public
prayer at a gathering in Knibb's home, the slave was arrested.
He was forced to lie on the ground, naked, held down by
four men, while twenty lashes with a bull whip were received upon his bleeding back. He then was chained to a
convict and made to walk in the hot sun to the fields, where,
as a member of a chain gang, he was made to work at hard
labor for two weeks.

William Knibb walked beside him. He took his hand as
they went down the road together, and lifted his spirits with
the assurance that God's grace would be sufficient for him.

In Knibb the slaveholders had challenged a gospel
preacher of iron will, one who would be more than a match
for them. His preaching and teaching were signally blessed.
His work for Christ went forward on waves of triumph.

When Knibb became pastor of a church of nine hundred
members in Falmouth, Jamaica, the infuriated planters renewed their war against him. They answered his antislavery
sermons by arranging public meetings at which they and
their cohorts denounced the missionaries as "infuriated luna-
tics." These meetings had influence with the public, for
most of the planters were not only rich and in control of the

newspapers, but also vestrymen in the Anglican Church.

Some of the slaveholders, despite their profession of Christianity, declared that they would kill their slaves before they would consent to grant them freedom. The knowledge that they were thus threatened with death caused some of the slaves to revolt. All this, of course, was blamed upon William Knibb.

At last the slavery forces succeeded in getting Knibb arrested and imprisoned. He had been urged by his friends to escape the island and he had had an opportunity to do so, but he had remained to face the danger. He would "take the consequences," as he had said.

Under the wave of persecution inspired by the slaveholders, his chapels and schools were wrecked and burned, as also were many of the homes of the Christian slaves. Finally Knibb's mission and work were prohibited by a law which the slaveholders succeeded in getting passed.

But his imprisonment gave William Knibb an opportunity to think out a determined plan of action for the future. He now resolved that he would have no rest or peace of mind until he had fought the slaveholders to a finish, and had freed every last slave among the 30,000 on the island.

As soon as Knibb's prison term ended, he hurriedly took ship for England. He escaped by a hair's breadth, for twenty conspirators had taken an oath that they would kill him as soon as he was freed from jail. But God spared Knibb, for God had a great work waiting for him to do in England.

Knibb planned to arouse his fellow Baptists, and indeed all his countrymen, against the iniquitous slave trade in the Caribbean Islands. He embarked on the greatest mission of his life, to secure the emancipation of these thousands of slaves. He resolved that in his lifetime he would hear their cheers of freedom.

Landing in England in 1832 at the age of twenty-nine, Knibb first met with the executive committee of the Baptist Missionary Society which supported him. When they confronted this antislavery reformer, the members of the committee at first were resolved to urge him to maintain a "hush-hush" policy about slavery. They advised him to keep silent.

Slavery, they said, was a political issue. The Missionary Society ought to concentrate on converting sinners, and keep out of such problems as slavery.

In answer to this, Knibb rose to his feet, bravely looked the cautious brethren straight in the eye and declared fervently: "My wife, my children, and I are entirely dependent on the Baptist mission. We have landed here without a shilling, but if necessary I will take my wife and children by the hand and I will walk barefoot throughout the length and breadth of the United Kingdom to make known to the Christians of England what their brethren in Jamaica are suffering."

The executive committee had had its warning. Here was a man who could not be silenced.

Although some Baptist preachers, before this time, had preached against slavery, and Robert Robinson, pastor of the church of Cambridge, had presented to the British House of Commons the first petition against the slave trade, William Knibb was the one Baptist who had fought the nefarious system on its own territory and was ablaze with a determined plan to eradicate the hellish trade.

A few days after his session with the executive committee, Knibb attended the annual meeting of the Missionary Society, for which an immense crowd had gathered. Many earnest sermons were preached, many emotional appeals were sounded, but never a reference was made to the curse of slavery. This disgraceful silence in the face of a terrible evil was too much for Knibb to take. His muscles quivered with the felt pain of the Baptist slaves who, at that very moment, were being flogged, while their homes were being burned as a punishment for praying.

Knibb rose to speak, and as he denounced the slave trade, the fire in his soul flamed up in impassioned eloquence. One of the worried, cautious British pastors clutched his coat tails and tried to pull him down, or at least to warn him to lay off the subject.

Yanking himself free from this timid fellow Baptist, Knibb persisted: "I will speak! At the risk of the severing of my connection with the society and the loss of all I hold dear, 103

I will avow this, and if the friends of missions will not hear me I will turn and tell it to my God! Nor will I desist till this greatest of all curses is removed and 'Glory to God in the highest!' is inscribed on the British flag!"

His intense sincerity electrified the large audience of Baptists. Then, for two whole years, Knibb expended his energies in a one-man campaign to arouse public opinion to break the shackles of the slaves. As if upborne by superhuman energy, he traveled the length and breadth of England and Scotland, conducting public rallies. By his burning zeal and eloquence, he roused vast numbers to fever pitch against slavery. Such a moral and social campaign had never before been carried forward by one man.

Throughout the British Isles audiences gave Knibb a deafening applause. They left no doubt that they vehemently shared his abhorrence of slavery, and that they supported his demand for its abolition by British law.

On these speaking tours, Knibb was often accompanied by Eustace Carey, a nephew of William Carey, the pioneer Baptist missionary. Eustace Carey has thus graphically described the power of young Knibb: "I witnessed congregated masses burning and almost raving with indignation at the slave system, as Knibb depicted its cruelties and demonstrated its crimes. His tact and self-possession became so remarkable that he would easily convert adverse occurrences into occasions of triumph for his cause."

Knibb was winning his fight. The British Parliament debated a bill to abolish slavery. Soon they enacted a bill abolishing colonial slavery, and set midnight July 31, 1833, as the hour when, by British law, the slaves should be declared formally and finally free.

As Knibb continued to plead his cause, Parliament also agreed to pay a large sum of money, by way of restitution, toward the rebuilding of the chapels, churches, and homes in Jamaica that had been destroyed.

Knibb, almost overcome with joy, hurried back to the island of Jamaica. He wanted to be there on the midnight of July 31, 1833, to share in the grand celebration of the emancipation of the slaves.

He was welcomed back with tremendous enthusiasm, amid scenes of indescribable joy and affection. Only the planters, whom he had defeated, were sullen with hate, bitter with humiliation.

Despite their vows that Knibb should never return to the island, he stood there on that joyous night, triumphant, surrounded by a vast throng of Negroes. As the midnight hour approached, he said, "The cruel monster is dying." Then, as the clock began to strike twelve, he shouted: "The monster is dead! The Negro is free! Thanks be to God!"

William Knibb's great work was done. He had fought a good fight and had lived to witness the hour of triumph. He had heard the exultant shout of men set free, a cry of joy such as is heard only from the throats of ransomed slaves.

Shortly, yellow fever struck Knibb down. The attack proved fatal, and though he died at the early age of forty-two, he had achieved a great life's work. He had accomplished more than do most men in twice that number of years.

More than eight thousand people attended his funeral services. Across the island the redeemed slaves sobbed:

"Massa Knibb dead!"

"He has gone to be with his brother, Tom," said his wife and children.

The historians say he was a young but immortal emancipator.

To that, his fellow Baptists add, "No Baptist was nobler or more worthy of the name."

CHAPTER 11

JOHN ALBERT BROADUS

Notable Preacher, Teacher, Scholar

IN GREENVILLE, S. C., two young theological professors stood on the steps of the Southern Baptist Seminary building. The year was 1865, and the War Between the States had just ended. "With Lee's surrender at Appomattox Courthouse and the soldiers returning homeward, we can reopen our work at the seminary, even though it must be in a small way and under some handicaps," said President James Boyce. "Yes," said John Albert Broadus. "I have been preparing a course of lectures on preaching in anticipation of a class in homiletics when we resume our work."

"Very good," said the president, "but I regret to inform you that you will have only one student in your homiletics class, and this student unfortunately is blind."

"I am indeed sorry to hear of his blindness," said Broadus, "but I assure you it will make no difference to me. I shall give him my best and I shall pursue my lectures as planned."

So day after day, to one blind student, Dr. Broadus gave the lectures on preaching which afterward were published as a book — a book which for more than half a century has been recognized everywhere as a classic in its field. *The Preparation and Delivery of Sermons,* by Broadus, has gone through fifty editions!

This human compassion to one blind student was typical of the acts, the character, and the stature of this man who endeared himself to the millions of Baptists throughout the United States.

Dr. Broadus was born in Culpeper County, Va., on January 24, 1827. His father, Edmund Broadus, although not a minister, came from a family of preachers, and was exceptionally intelligent and devout. In addition to owning a small farm, he was prominent in the Virginia legislature and held a commission as major in the Culpeper militia.

An uncle by the name of Albert G. Sims seems to have been his early tutor and teacher. In fact, his schooling was somewhat irregular until he entered the University of Virginia, where after four years of disciplined study he received the degree of Master of Arts. He did not attend any theological school, because no theological school existed among the Baptists of the South at that time. Yet he became, for thirty-six years, the best known and most respected professor of what came to be the leading theological seminary among Baptists in the South. He was a natural-born scholar who had the initiative for a self-directed study. He disciplined himself in Greek and Hebrew, and much of his education was due to his independent and ambitious pursuit of scholarship.

John A. Broadus was won to Christ when he was about sixteen years of age. He had grown up, of course, in a religious home where the environment was one of devotion. Yet he had his own decision to make. In a revival service at the Mount Poney Baptist Church, he was deeply moved by a sermon from the text, "All that the Father giveth me shall come to me; and him that cometh to me I will in no wise cast out." As the preacher gave the invitation, young John came under conviction, but he hesitated to go forward. A friend in the pew behind him leaned forward and, putting a hand on the young lad's shoulder, whispered, "Right now, won't you accept this promise of Christ, and give your heart and life to him?" With this encouragement, the lad left his seat and went down the aisle in full surrender to Christ.

The next day he heard S. M. Poindexter preach on the Parable of the Talents. Broadus was deeply moved by a call to the ministry. He went to see his pastor and said, "Brother Grimsley, I have been thinking of preparing to study medicine. But somehow I know that God has called me to preach the gospel. The question is decided, I must try to be a preacher."

Following his graduation from the University of Virginia, where he majored in Greek, he taught Greek for a time. He then received a call to become pastor of the Baptist church in Charlottesville, Va., where the University of Virginia is located. This was a most fortunate circumstance, for there he was under the necessity of preaching the gospel with high thinking expressed in simple form. He had to meet the challenge of preaching to five distinct groups in his church. There were the professors from the university, the merchants and businessmen of the town, the farmers from the outlying rural section, the children who were a part of his congregation, and the large number of slaves who sat in the gallery. This would be a difficult challenge to any preacher!

The need to proclaim the gospel with sufficient simplicity to be understood by children and slaves, and yet with such scholarship as to challenge the minds and hearts of university professors, called forth his genius. As a result, perhaps more than any other preacher in America, Broadus mastered the art of studied simplicity combined with effective power in preaching. Sometimes those who heard him for the first time went away disappointed, because they had expected something more dramatic and sensational. Then they discovered that just because his sermons had been so clear and simple, they could not forget them. They always came back again to be profoundly moved.

But though Broadus loved preaching, he was destined to become a teacher of preachers. While North and South were astir with agitation over the slavery question and the tensions around him were mounting, he quietly joined the first faculty of the Southern Baptist Theological Seminary when it opened in Greenville, S. C., in 1859. It was here, after the war had ended, that he delivered to the one blind student his famous lectures on preaching. Later, when the seminary moved to Louisville, Ky., Broadus continued to preach and teach. He served as a professor for a total of thirty-six years.

During the War Between the States, he served as a chap-

lain in General Lee's army. His letters give a vivid description of the hundreds of soldiers who gathered about him, often deeply moved to tears as he preached to them with his direct simplicity and sincere passion. He vividly describes standing in sorrow in Winchester, Va., as the litters of wounded soldiers were borne past him after the Battle of Gettysburg. The scenes of the war cut deeply into his heart, but at the same time they helped him to preach with a more gripping reality, because he had to learn to preach to men who were facing death daily in the Armed Forces of the Confederacy. Some of his biographers think that Broadus did his best preaching to the soldiers. Said Dr. J. Williams Jones, "I never heard him preach with such beautiful simplicity and thrilling power the old gospel that he loves so well."

Dr. Broadus, despite his scholarly labors upon such works as *A Harmony of the Gospels,* never lost his fine sense of humor. After he had published his large and important *Commentary of the Gospel of Matthew,* he met on the street one day one of his Negro minister friends. In a jovial way he said to his friend:

"Brother Smith, how did you like that commentary on Matthew's Gospel which I gave you?"

"Well, Brother Broadus," answered the Negro preacher, "I must say that the Bible throws great light on your commentary."

He often lighted his sermons with flashes of kindly humor. With nimble wit he once remarked, "The best committee is a committee of three — with one sick and one out of town."

Because of Dr. Broadus' mastery of the art of preaching, the Divinity School of Yale University asked him to deliver the famous Lyman Beecher Lectures on Preaching. Broadus was the first and only Southern Baptist minister ever asked to give this notable series of lectures.

Love of children was characteristic of him. He encouraged them to be present in his congregation, and he knew how to talk to them in an entertaining manner. "He loved to have his own children sit in the study while he worked," wrote his close friend, Dr. A. T. Robertson. "They could see his zeal in consulting commentaries, dictionaries, and grammars." One day a ten-year-old boy listened to Dr. Broadus preach on the subject, "The Practical Aspect of the Trinity." Dr. Broadus was proud and gratified when the lad said to him at the close of the service, "Dr. Broadus that was a delightful sermon that you gave us on the Trinity."

Children always responded with special love for him. They still tell in Louisville the story of a young boy who was reported lost on a Sunday night. Alarmed parents sent neighbors and police in search of him. Later in the night he turned up on his own. "Where have you been?" demanded the exasperated parents." "I went to hear Dr. Broadus preach," was the simple answer.

For children he prepared, *A Catechism of Bible Teaching*. In terse sentences, it gave boys and girls clear answers to theological questions.

In his preaching, some rural folk missed in the conversational style of Broadus what they called the sacred "whangdoodle" and which others have called "the holy whine." Because he regarded his voice as important, he took elocution lessons to employ it to best advantage. His voice was both rich and penetrating, with great ranges of tenderness and sympathy. Yet, when occasion demanded, he could raise his voice to denunciation and to the powerful effect of an explosive moment.

Scholar, teacher, and preacher, Broadus held reverently to the Bible. "Be willing to let the Bible mean what it wants to mean," he advised. "If you forget everything else I have told you, don't forget to read the Scriptures in a commonsense way." He had quips for his young fellow preachers too. "Some preachers get their texts from the Bible," he said, "and their sermons from the newspapers." In the very last lecture he gave, he pleaded with his students to be like Apollos, "mighty in the scriptures."

Dr. Broadus never had more than uncertain health in a body none too strong. His severe application to his books and his studies tended to subtract from his health. But he learned to preserve his strength, and he lived actively until sixty-eight years of age. He got a great deal of exercise by walking. Indeed, he is said to have worn a path walking back and forth preparing his sermons.

Broadus excelled as a preacher and he never wanted for great crowds to flock to his preaching. As Robertson has so well said: "The preaching of Broadus matched with the highest order of genius the ripest scholarship. . . . His true place is with the great preachers of the second half of the nineteenth century."

CHAPTER 12

JOHN E. CLOUGH

Missionary Extraordinary

ON AN IOWA FARM near the close of the Civil War, a young man was standing on a four-horse reaper breaking off the heavy grain when one of the farm hands came across the field. As he approached, he called out, "Here's a letter for you from Boston." John Clough seated himself on the reaper, tied the reins around the seat, and tore open the letter. As he read, his eyes widened with surprise. Then a broad smile came upon his face. He shouted to his associates, waving the letter as he did so: "What do you know! They want me to go to India as a missionary! It's a call from the Baptist Foreign Mission Board in Boston."

Little did that farmer know that, in the providence of God, he was destined to reap a harvest greater by far than any harvest of wheat or corn in Iowa.

But John Clough was more than a farmer. He was an educated man who had been head of a public school and who had served as a leader in politics. More recently, he had felt called to religious service, and he had been working for the American Baptist Publication Society as a colporteur in the Middle West. At times, the thought of becoming a lawyer had fired his imagination, but that idea had never wholly satisfied him. Then, when he attended a Baptist Convention in Davenport, Iowa, an address by a missionary to the Chinese in Bangkok, Siam, deeply stirred him. Clough's soul became aflame and he exclaimed, half aloud: "This is my call! I recognize it! Now I know where God wants me!"

In his earlier youth, however, Clough had shown little interest in religion. At college he had let it be known to his classmates that they could count him out of any religious practices. Every night his roommate read a chapter of the Bible and tried to pray with him. Clough did not like this and proposed that they draw a chalk line through the middle of the room with the understanding that on one side his religious roommate could pray if he wished to do so, but on the other side Clough would be left free to study undisturbed by Christian devotions.

While Clough was a student at Upper Iowa University, the president one day invited him to attend his Sunday Bible class at the Baptist church. Slowly but effectually the Spirit of God broke down young Clough's professed resistance. One evening he found it difficult to keep his attention on his studies. He pushed aside his books, stepped softly over the chalk line, and knelt beside his praying roommate. Shortly after this, under the guidance of Pastor Johnson, Clough was led to baptism in the First Baptist Church of Burlington, Iowa.

After reading the letter which he had opened while on the reaper in the wheat field, Clough made a visit to Boston to meet the officers of the Missionary Board. There he agreed to accept an appointment to India. It was to the difficult Telugu Mission, known as the "Forlorn Hope." It had been so named because after many years it had shown such small results that on three different occasions the board had considered closing it and crossing it off as a failure. Yet, undaunted, the missionaries on the field, chief of whom was Dr. Lyman Jewett, had pleaded that the mission, despite some seventeen years of apparent failure, might be continued for a while longer.

Iowa friends of Clough were astounded by his adventurous decision to undertake this almost hopeless task in India. Some members of his family were particularly angry with him. His brothers and sisters thought him crazy. Many of his friends said: "You are throwing your life away. You had a chance to be a strong leader here in the state of Iowa. Now you have decided to bury yourself in faraway India."

Nevertheless, on November 30, 1864, the resolute John E. Clough and his brave wife set sail from Boston on a little ship called the "James Guthrie." This ship, of only eight hundred tons, was scarcely seaworthy. It rolled and pitched unmercifully and narrowly missed drifting into wrecks as it rounded the Cape of Good Hope. For food, the Cloughs had corn-meal mush with molasses at nearly every meal; for an exquisite delicacy, they sometimes had an Irish potato!

The Cloughs did not arrive in India until almost the first of April. Then they journeyed, by slow stages, on a spring-less bullock cart to the mission station at Nellore, where they arrived on April 22, 1865. From Nellore, Clough and Jewett traveled the seventy-six miles to Ongole, where it was planned that Clough should open a new mission station. Clough desired not only to talk with a man of the Madiga tribe who was inquiring the way to Christ, but also to visit the place which has now come to be known as Prayer Meeting Hill.

On this hill just back of Ongole, on New Year's Day, 1854, Jewett and his native helpers had held a memorable prayer meeting. They had selected that hill as a suitable place where they might plead with God to send a missionary through whom the barrenness of that mission field might be changed into fruitfulness. Arriving at that place of prayer at 4:00 A.M., they read as a Scripture passage Isaiah, chapter 52, which includes the words: "How beautiful upon the mountains are the feet of him that bringeth good tidings, that publisheth peace." Then they had earnestly prayed together. Just as they concluded their prayer meeting, the sun arose. This seemed to be a sign of God's answer. Now, eleven years after that famous prayer meeting, John E. Clough placed his feet firmly on the hill in Ongole and the work on the Telugu mission field was begun.

Strangely enough, Clough's coming to Ongole had really been made possible by the reading of a poem written by the Rev. S. F. Smith, the man who wrote the hymn, "My Country 'Tis of Thee." The Baptist Missionary Union in the United States, at its annual meeting, which in 1853 was held in Albany, N. Y., was minded to abandon the Telugu field, which had become known as "The Lone Star Mission." Many could see no future for it. All through the night preceding the session when the matter was to be put to a vote, Smith could not sleep. In his concern, he rose from his bed and wrote a poem which he entitled, "Lone Star."

The next morning this poem was read to the assembled Mission Board, and the members were so moved that they wept. Something about the last stanza of the poem seemed prophetic.

> Shine on, "Lone Star!" till earth redeemed,
> In dust shall bid its idols fall;
> And thousands, where thy radiance beamed,
> Shall "crown the Saviour, Lord of all."

At once, with tear-filled eyes, the board members voted not to abandon, but rather, to strengthen the Telugu mission. This is how Clough, a decade and more later, came to be sent to this long-barren field.

Clough undertook the difficult work of the mission sustained by an indomitable spirit and inspired by an intense love of humble people. He possessed a genius for organization and the faculty to make wise decisions. He was a masterful missionary leader through whom God achieved astonishing results.

In order to undergird the future of the mission field at Ongole, Clough had to make three crucial decisions. He prayerfully faced the problem of Indian caste in relation to the mission church. The higher social group of Indians let him know that they would not become Christians if in the church they would have to associate with outcaste people who sometimes ate carrion. Clough asked himself, "Must I forbid the outcaste people to come to Christ in order to receive into membership some of the high caste people?" It was an old and difficult problem. To this day it plagues many churches not in India only, but also in the United States. Then a strange thing happened. As Clough prayed for light, he opened his Bible at random and the text of 1 Corinthians 1:26-29 was before his eyes. At about the same time in another room, Mrs. Clough opened her Bible and her eyes fell on precisely the same text. Clough interpreted

116

this double event as more than coincidence. To him it was divine guidance. He rejected the introduction of castes into the Baptist church in India. He would not tolerate a segregated church. The outcastes were to be welcome to come to Christ, as were people of every caste, if they were willing to join a church in which all should be one in Christ Jesus.

The second decision came because of the great famine of 1876-1878. With the compassion of the Christ who fed the five thousand, Clough threw all his energies into feeding the hungry and driving away the wolf of starvation. His appeals in England and the United States for famine relief money met a generous response and he fed the hungry with great personal sacrifice and devotion.

The third decision was to procure from the government a contract to build a canal. This enabled him to provide work for the famishing, during the prolonged period of famine. The government yielded to his pleas and let him put hundreds of people to work digging a canal three and one-half miles long, now called the Buckingham Canal. During rest periods, he had his Indian helpers preach to the workers.

Many of the natives, moved by his preaching of the gospel and convinced of his sincerity by his works of mercy, desired to become Christians. For fifteen months, Clough refused to baptize them, for he did not want "rice Christians" in the church. But careful examination, one by one, of these applicants for baptism convinced him of their sincerity. They had waited to confess Christ as long as he dared to hold them back.

Accordingly, Clough one day stood under a grove of trees on the bank and supervised his ordained native preachers as they baptized great numbers in the river Gundlacumma. That was a day above all others, one never to be forgotten. It was indeed a modern Pentecost. The baptizing started at 6 A.M. when two preachers began immersing converts. When the preachers became tired, they were relieved by two other preachers. By five o'clock that afternoon, 2,222 had been buried with Christ in baptism. They continued to baptize for the next two days. In a three-day period, while Clough directed operations, six Indian pastors baptized a total of 3,536 Indian converts, more than were baptized on the day of Pentecost.

In 1879, Clough and his helpers toured among the villages that were not too distant, and continued their baptizing of converts. In thirty-nine days they baptized altogether 8,691. During this time, Clough ordained twenty-four Telugu preachers. So amazing was the revival movement that by 1882 there were 20,865 Christians connected with the Ongole field.

After Clough had completed forty years of unparalleled success as a missionary the ill health which was to be expected when one worked in India, overtook him. He died in Rochester, N. Y., in November, 1910. The Iowa man on the reaper had reaped a harvest the size of which he had not dreamed and which in numbers of converts has not been equalled by any Protestant mission in a like period of time. His body was buried in Newton Centre, Mass., close to the grave of Dr. S. F. Smith who had written the poem which had saved the Ongole mission.

Today there is in Ongole a hospital of 250 beds, known as the Clough Memorial Hospital. A girls' school in Ongole is serving to educate scores of Indian girls. It is a memorial to Mrs. Clough. In addition to these two institutions which memorialize the Cloughs, his descendants have held aloft the missionary torch. The Reverend John Martin, a grandson, is an American Baptist missionary who is ably serving in the Ongole area. Mrs. Leon Roland, a granddaughter, is a missionary in the Telugu field. Thus, the work of this extraordinary missionary has been continued through the years.

Clough was indeed "a driving, rushing, torrential leader" — a missionary extraordinary.

CHAPTER 13

CHARLES HADDON SPURGEON

Prince of Preachers

THERE WAS SUCH A BIG SNOW storm that Sunday morning in Colchester, England, that the fifteen-year-old boy was stopped in his tracks. To escape the storm, he took refuge in a chapel on a side street. Not more than a dozen persons had gathered for worship that morning, and no one of them particularly noticed the boy who, being a stranger, cautiously slipped into one of the back pews. Neither did the tall, thin, shoe-maker preacher, who was pinch-hitting for the absent pastor, know that his text, "Look unto me, and be ye saved, all the ends of the earth," would set off an emotional explosion in the heart of the young stranger.

"I remember the hour," Charles Haddon Spurgeon wrote afterward. It all had happened quietly, yet it proved to be the crucial moment that transformed the lad's life. Fixing his eyes upon him, the lay preacher had said, "You are in trouble, young man, and you'll never get out of it unless you look to Jesus." Then, lifting up his hands, he had shouted, "Look! Look! Look!"

Young Spurgeon at that moment did look up to Christ and found him as his Savior and Lord. Little did that preacher to a handful of people on that wintry morning guess that a miracle had taken place in a young man's life — a miracle of grace which would set off dynamic and world-wide influences.

This conversion experience relieved the boy's spirit of great mental anguish and sharp disturbance of conscience. Now he knew himself as a happy and changed person.

This lad, in later years, would preach to tens of thousands in a great church in London. His sermons, translated into many languages, would be read by millions, and he would become known as the most famous preacher the Baptists had ever given to the world.

His parents, who were Congregationalists, were taken by surprise when young Spurgeon announced his baptism. Family prayers and daily Bible reading were part of his home background. His father and grandfather before him were preachers, and young Spurgeon knew how to study the Bible for himself. Like Judson, he thereby became a convinced Baptist and was baptized on May 3, 1851, on his mother's birthday in the river Lark at a quiet spot a half-mile from the village of Isleham. The first brave flowers of spring were lifting their heads along the river bank, but the morning was so cold that the church people had built a fire of peat by whose glowing coals they tried to keep warm. Sixteen-year-old Charles had been up since very early morning, for he had walked the eight long miles to the place of baptism.

"I had often prayed the Lord that you might be converted," his mother said, "but I never asked him that you might be a Baptist!"

An avid reader, young Spurgeon devoured the books in the libraries of his father and grandfather and learned to read the Greek New Testament. In later years he would acquire a great library. For a number of years, he went to secondary school. He wanted to attend the University of Cambridge, but that historic university barred the entrance of Baptists. Accordingly, he studied hard on his own and worked for a time as an assistant schoolmaster.

Seemingly blocked in his efforts to go to college, he heard the call to preach and, at only eighteen years of age, he pastored the church at Waterbeach. "I am bound to give myself unto reading, study, and prayer" he resolved, "not to grieve the Spirit by unthought-of effusion." Under his magnetic preaching the congregation of twenty at Waterbeach grew to four hundred. Two years later, his preaching power won him an urgent call to a London church. Here, the crowds attending upon his preaching gave unquestioned proof of his ministry. He was called "mad" because he ventured to build in London the Metropolitan Baptist Tabernacle, seating 5,000 persons. "He can never fill all those pews," pessimists predicted, wagging their heads for emphasis; but fill them he did for thirty-seven years, and everywhere, as his fame spread, people loudly demanded copies of his sermons that they might read them.

Charles Haddon Spurgeon

Responding to this urgent request, he published his sermons weekly for forty years and they were widely distributed in Europe, England, and America. They sold the incredible figure of 150 million copies.

However, Spurgeon's fearless preaching against slavery met with rebuff in our Southland where his sermons once had been so popular. As a consequence of his strong stand for the freedom of the slaves, his books for over ten years were boycotted, banned, and in some cases burned in the South.

With prolific pen he produced books, commentaries, and sermons, while translators made many of his works available in the European languages, including Russian. In all, he wrote 135 books — a forty-foot shelf.

The enduring popularity of his work is marked by the fact that the last book to be published by the religious press in China before the Communists shut down Christian publication was Spurgeon's book, *Morning by Morning*. His world-wide influence is still a living power.

Spurgeon was short (five feet, six inches), stocky, with beard, brown eyes, heavy shock of hair, large mouth, richly melodious voice, fluent and eloquent of speech. Passion of heart, love of sinners, and flaming desire to win people to Christ were the secrets of his pulpit ministry. He regularly used simple, sinewy Anglo-Saxon words in his preaching, and his ideas were graphically enforced with homely illustrations. Doubtless because he preached to be understood and to be persuasive, many of his fellow ministers who preferred "polysyllabic Latinizations" thought him a heretic. They could not countenance a preacher who, by a touch of irony or humor, would lead his congregation to laughter — in a church! Perhaps those who preached to half-empty pews envied this man who held five thousand spellbound Sunday after Sunday. Naturally, they concluded that such a preacher must be a sensationalist.

The triumphs which attended Spurgeon's ministry were not without a share of pain and tragedy. Soon after his coming to London, he engaged for his services Surrey Music Hall, which seated ten thousand, the largest in London. A great crowd packed the place. The meeting had only been in progress a few minutes when someone cried "Fire! The galleries are giving way!" The vast throng stampeded in panic for the doors. Many were crushed under foot. Seven were killed and not a few seriously injured. The grief over this tragedy became a recurring depression complex in Spurgon's life.

Then too, his wife became a bedridden invalid for a score of years, while he himself, over a period of years, had bouts with painful illnesses which on occasion kept him out of his pulpit and sent him for recuperation to the south of France for two or three months at a time. Also the financial burdens of the institutions he founded and maintained weighed heavily upon him, not to mention the mental anguish and the physical strain of knowing that thousands week by week were hanging upon his every word. In his deep moods of depression, however, he discovered the divine blessings, for he said: "Depression comes over me whenever the Lord is preparing a larger blessing for my ministry. It has now become to me a prophet in rough clothing."

Meanwhile, Spurgeon, as a true minister of the gospel, felt the tug and pull of human need around him. He heard the cry of orphans and founded a home for fatherless children — Stockwell Orphanage with five hundred children.

The plight of the aged led him to establish a pension fund and housing for the needy aged — The Metropolitan Alms-houses. Denied the privilege of a full education himself, he founded a training college for ministers, called the Pastor's College. With evangelistic zeal, he organized ninety colporteurs to sell Bibles and Christian literature. He built new

Baptist churches and inspired the sending out of scores of missionaries. The Metropolitan Baptist Tabernacle became a center of spiritual power; it radiated waves of grace which touched multitudes of human hearts in many lands. The bombers which flew over London in World War II left Spurgeon's Tabernacle a hollow shell of ruins, but so vital still is Spurgeon's influence that the great church has been rebuilt and its ministry goes on.

On Sunday, June 7, 1891, Spurgeon preached as a broken man. Though but fifty-six years of age, he was so weak that he had to support himself with his right hand on the chair. Many in the congregation felt that this was the last time they would hear his golden voice. Rushed to France, he grew steadily worse. He sent a last loving cabled message to the members of his church. To his secretary he sighed, "My work is done." Sixty thousand persons attended his funeral.

Baptists have had only one Charles Haddon Spurgeon, and indeed, this might be said for all of English Protestantism. In three generations, no other preacher has had so wide an audience or so permanent an influence. He gave steady pastoral and institutional leadership for forty years, and his sermons circulated throughout all Christendom, a record that remains unequalled.

The strange boy in the back pew in that little Primitive Methodist Chapel on that stormy Sunday morning, by the grace of God, became a magnificent voice that proclaimed the gospel with unparalled evangelistic effectiveness. His motto was "He that winneth souls is wise." In that wisdom Spurgeon excelled.

CHAPTER 14

RUSSELL H. CONWELL

Lawyer-Preacher and Builder

THE TALL BOSTON LAWYER looked across his desk at his Baptist visitor, Mrs. Barrett of Lexington. Politely, but firmly, he tried to conclude the interview.

"Mrs. Barrett," he said in his rich baritone voice, "with so few church members left and the church building so dilapidated, I can see no way out of your problem except to sell the church property. You can, of course, give the money from the sale to some worthy Baptist cause."

Mrs. Barrett looked grim. "But, Mr. Conwell," she objected, "we have two or three deacons who will never vote to sell the church, no matter what comes to pass. After all, a few yards beyond our church is the village green where our fathers fought the British Redcoats in the battle of Lexington — the first armed resistance of the Revolution — and somehow we feel it would be a disgrace not to hold on."

"I hadn't thought of that," said Conwell, cupping his chin in his hands. "Lexington does indeed display a spirit of proud determination. But what can you do?"

"Well," Mrs. Barrett answered coyly, for she discerned that she had struck a spark, "if you would just come out and speak to us next Sunday and see things for yourself, that might help."

"I'll do it," said the lawyer, as he rose to lead his client to the door. "Count on me to be there. You see how many people you can get out."

124 "Oh, thank you, Mr. Conwell. We'll do our best."

Their best was only eighteen people; they could muster no more. But those few awakened a flame of burning desire in the soul of the Boston attorney. "I resolved that night after hours of struggle and prayer to my Lord — to at least dedicate myself to the cause [the ministry] which I should have adopted before. I dared not disobey the Divine Call."

Most men who enter the ministry do so in early life following college. Unlike them, Russell H. Conwell was now thirty-seven years old and secure in a leading profession in a big city. In his case, to become a preacher in middle life meant the abandonment of the lucrative profession of law; it meant accepting the hazards of serving a poverty-stricken church in whose treasury was the sum total of $1.50. No wonder his friends thought that his decision was the sign of an unbalanced mind!

The next Sunday at Lexington, however, Conwell did not lack for evidence that his decision had been wise. The church was so crowded that some people had to stand on the church steps and on the sidewalk. They wanted to hear this Boston lawyer, this ex-army colonel, now turned preacher to a rundown Baptist church. Actually, the weight of the crowd broke down the church steps — a most fortunate accident, as it turned out. The steps could not remain unrepaired with a man of such direct action as Conwell on hand. On Monday morning, those living neighbor to the church witnessed Conwell at work with saw and hammer rebuilding the church steps and porch. Businessmen hurrying to the commuter's train for Boston, stopped long enough to inquire, "What's going on here?"

"I'm getting ready to build a new Baptist church," said Conwell with smiling conviction. The very first passerby said, "Well, here's $100 to help you." Nearly all who passed by gave something, and before long Conwell had $5,000 in hand toward a new church. In one and a half years, with the help of his congregation, he dedicated the new Lexington Baptist Church.

A few years ago, when I preached in this church, I reverently paused on the steps to view in my imagination the figure of Russell Conwell, wearing a carpenter's apron and

125

down on his knees repairing the steps. Here was a minister who meant business, with no fooling and no time wasted.

Of course, when a man is not afraid to tackle a hard job, word of it gets around. Before long, a church in sad plight in Philadelphia appealed to Conwell to come and help it.

This Philadelphia church was so deeply in debt that the sheriff had moved to foreclose on the mortgage. The group was pathetically small and discouraged, and their financial obligations were large for those days. Indeed, the church was on the verge of complete failure. But this type of tough situation had special appeal to a man of Conwell's powers. He accepted the call to the Philadelphia pastorate.

Again, as in Lexington, the crowds came. The seating capacity of the Grace Baptist Church, of which Conwell had become pastor, was increased to twelve hundred, but still people were turned away. With more people being turned away each Sunday, Conwell knew that he must build a much larger church. Forthwith he proposed to build, with the help of God, a Baptist Temple which would seat over three thousand, one hundred persons. Timid and envious persons called his project "mad folly." Besides, there were enormous financial barriers to his project. In the genius of the historic Baptist mission to the world, Conwell was preaching to the common people and his congregation was made up of the small wage earners. There was not one rich person in the church. The money would have to be raised by sacrifices. "Walking Clubs" were organized to save street car fares. Men gave up tobacco to give more money to the building fund. But with all the plans of money raising, it was the sacrifice of a child, Hattie Wyatt, that really put the great building project on its feet.

The story was written by a member of Dr. Conwell's church and Dr. Conwell said that it was true to the facts.

Hattie Wyatt, only six years old, wore her best starched dress as she tripped along on her way to Sunday school. She was gay of heart to be actually going at last to the Sunday school of the Grace Baptist Church. But she was utterly crushed when she reached the church. She was turned away solely because there was no room in the overcrowded building for her. She sobbed brokenheartedly all her slow, lonely walk home.

That night as she said her goodnight prayer by her bed, her mother heard her pray that God would make room enough for her so that she could go to the Sunday school.

No one knows (except those who do not underestimate the power of the Holy Spirit in the life of a child) how it came about that the next morning she conceived the childish idea that she could build a larger Sunday school, if only she were careful to save enough pennies. Her childlike faith, of course, knew nothing of the cost of such a building. Now, one of her cherished keepsakes was a little red pocketbook, and into this tiny treasury one by one, day by day, week by week, she stored her hard-to-come-by pennies.

It was only a few weeks after she had begun her penny saving that a fatal illness fastened upon her frail little body. A galloping sickness wasted away her strength. Perhaps the sad look on her mother's face or the hushed voices in her room gave her sensitive spirit awareness that whatever she was to do, she must do quickly. She called her mother to her bedside. "Get me my little red pocketbook in the bureau drawer, will you, mother?" she asked. The mother brought the pocketbook and put it in her child's thin, white hands. Too weak to count the pennies herself, she said, "You count the pennies for me, please." Putting the pennies one by one on the bedspread, they together counted fifty-seven pennies. It was then that Hattie, with almost her dying breath, told her mother that these were the pennies she had saved in order to build a larger Sunday school for Dr. Conwell's church.

The next Sunday with broken voice and tear-filled eyes, Dr. Conwell held up Hattie Wyatt's little red pocketbook with its fifty-seven pennies and told her story. He saw his congregation melt to tears, and somehow he knew that they were not going to let Hattie Wyatt down.

Afterward, he wrote, "When we heard how God had blessed us with so great an inheritance, there was silence — a silence of tears and earnest consecration." He knew that in principle the cornerstone was laid, and a new temple erected 127 that very day by Hattie Wyatt's childlike faith and sacrifice.

Dr. Russell Conwell seemed always to achieve incredible results. He baptized 6,000 persons, and by his sermons and famous lectures, he addressed 10,000,000 hearers. A half-dozen biographies of famous men came from his pen. His book, *The Life of Charles H. Spurgeon,* sold 125,000 copies in the first four months. Its influence was so great that in a single month twenty-five young men sent to Dr. Conwell letters telling of their decision to enter the Christian ministry as a result of reading this book. Altogether, Conwell, busy as he was, found time to write nearly a score of books.

Always eager to help ambitious young men, Dr. Conwell undertook to tutor personally a young man by the name of Charles Davies who came to him wanting to study for the ministry. He agreed to teach him Latin and Greek for one hour on three evenings a week. Imagine how Conwell must have felt when this young man brought six other young men with him for the first evening. The word spread, and at the second meeting of this class, forty young men appeared, all wanting a wider education! Quickly Conwell organized an evening school with six volunteer teachers. This he followed with plans for a college (afterward a university). This institution, chartered in 1888, was named after the church, Temple University. Many now think that it should have been named Conwell University, as Harvard was named for its founder, John Harvard.

From this simple beginning of helping young men gain an eduation grew the great Temple University of Philadelphia. Today, this university enrolls 28,000 students. It has a faculty of one thousand members and a property worth millions of dollars.

But Conwell was to prove himself more than a great pastor, popular preacher, able teacher, church builder, and college founder. The sick, the maimed, and the needy that he encountered everywhere in the great city, appealed to his compassion. Such a man as Conwell could not rest without doing something about the problem of sickness among the poor. Conwell's concern led, as we shall presently see, to the founding of another great institution.

A young woman, an orphan, needing special medical attention, appealed to her pastor for help. Her disease was dangerous and infectious. With the co-operation of the physicians, Conwell rented two rooms in a private home and paid for a nurse to care for the woman. As before in the case of the evening school development, more cases of sick persons required more space. Under Conwell's guidance, therefore, there was developed the Good Samaritan Hospital (now Temple University Hospital), an organization which today represents a famous institution and ministers to thousands of the needy.

From the Baptist viewpoint, one sad note mars the founding of the college and the hospital. Conwell wanted the help of his own Baptist denomination (he had studied for a time at Newton Theological Institution) for these projects. Due to indifference or blindness, his fellow Baptists gave to these institutions little or no support and encouragement, and consequently prevented these famous institutions from becoming Baptist. In one of the largest cities in the nation, a great university and a great hospital might have belonged to the Baptists, if the Baptists had not been so strangely unresponsive to Conwell's outstanding leadership in these matters.

To the world at large, Conwell is best known, after the founding of these two institutions, for his famous lecture, "Acres of Diamonds." He delivered this lecture more than 6,100 times, and for it he collected large lecture fees. All of this money he turned back into the work of the church, the college, and the hospital, with the result that although he contributed upwards of five million dollars to these institutions, he died a poor man.

Dr. Conwell was voted the First Citizen of Philadelphia. As he went to the Academy of Music to attend a public reception in his honor, at which there were addresses by the governor and the mayor, the throngs who crowded the sidewalks of Broad Street made the area echo with their cheers.

He once had been a runaway boy, but the grace of God had made him a towering figure of national significance. His ministry lighted an undying torch of truth and illuminated

129

the minds of hundreds of thousands of students. His compassion put the healing hand of medical care upon thousands. His voice inspired and gave new hope to ten million souls. Here was indeed a great man.

CHAPTER 15

GEORGE W. TRUETT

World Baptist Leader

"ARE YOU GOOD AT ROPIN' and brandin' sinners?" asked a cowboy of George W. Truett, the Baptist preacher from Dallas, Texas. Truett had come to hold a camp meeting, a big event for which 2,500 cowboys gathered each year. As he was camping down for the night, he was surprised by the approach of a deputation of cowboys riding their horses. They arrived at his camping place just as he was finishing his supper. "Kayn yo' shoot quick, parson?" they asked. " 'Cause if yo' kayn't shoot quick, we reckon we all have sent for the wrong parson." It was the cowboys' way of saying that they wanted him to preach that very hour under the cottonwood trees. He did, and for many seasons more he was the cowboys' favorite preacher. His ministry there was blessed with many conversions.

He had to be a man of steady nerves, for sometimes drunken cowboys would come down the aisle toward the pulpit, whipping out their revolvers as they came. This Texas preacher always was able to handle even the roughest of the cattlemen, for he had a quiet but sincere way, and he was a tall, massive man with broad shoulders, stern face, and powerful muscles.

He knew by experience something about gun toting. It was a gun that had brought him the tragic experience which remade him as a great preacher. He had gone out hunting one day with a Texas Ranger, Captain J. C. Arnold, who was the chief of police of Dallas. They were returning home

132

from the hunt, with Arnold walking a few paces ahead of Truett. As Truett shifted his hammerless gun from one shoulder to another, the trigger was touched. The gun went off and wounded the man in front. It was a fatal wounding, for Arnold died in a few days.

The shock to Truett seemed irreparable. Arnold was his personal friend, a member of his church, and thus Truett carried on his conscience the death of his best friend as the result of a possibly careless act. Immediately he determined to give up preaching. It was only after a bitter struggle that he finally was encouraged to resume his pulpit work. The depth of his sorrow, however, from this time onward gave to his preaching a new tenderness, a new depth of sincerity, and a new power. The legend grew, however, that he never smiled again.

Crowds flocked to hear him in the First Baptist Church of Dallas, and this church soon had 8,000 members. Throughout the Southland and indeed throughout all the countries served by the Baptist World Alliance, he became the most famous preacher among the Baptists of his time. His magnificent qualities of character, together with his moving power as a preacher, meant that wherever he was announced, overflow crowds came to hear him.

In many ways his life was an extraordinary one, for from his earliest years, it was marked by his ability to make friends, to win confidence, and to convince people by his rare persuasive powers. Whenever he asked people to do something, they always seemed quick and willing to respond. He had power over people individually and likewise over multitudes.

In fact, it was because of this gift that Baylor University, when Truett was only twenty-three years of age and before he had himself attended college, called him to lead in a campaign to raise a huge sum of money needed to save the university from bankruptcy. His magnetic appeal and terrific persuasive power soon paid off the Baylor debt. Later, when he entered the university as a freshman, it was a unique experience in college history — granting entrance to a freshman who had been the savior of his college!

Young George Truett had grown up in the hills back in 133

North Carolina, where he had been born in 1867, two years after Grant and Lee had shaken hands at Appomattox Courthouse.

He was converted in his nineteenth year in a revival service in the Baptist Church House in Clay County, North Carolina. He had always attended Sunday school, and within him was the desire to get right with God.

The preacher's text one Sunday night was, "Now the just shall live by faith: and if any man draw back, my soul shall have no pleasure in him." The earnest words of the preacher were followed by an immediate invitation to accept Christ as personal Savior. George Truett was one of the young people who went forward that night. Truett put to himself this test the next morning: "Was he willing," he asked himself, "to do with his life from that time onward, and without evasion or reservation, whatever Christ might ask him to do?" Truett could answer from deep within himself an unreserved "Yes," and he said that as a result, a great peace filled his heart.

Dr. George W. Truett's ministry pushed far beyond the bounds of Dallas, Texas. He traveled on a world preaching tour among mission stations, and during World War I he proclaimed the gospel to our soldiers in France and England. He was a leading figure in the National Preaching Mission. Three times he was President of the Baptist World Alliance, and with Dr. Rushbrooke and others he brought relief, inspiration, and wider fellowship to Baptists in many countries.

In his World War I service, on one occasion he was entertained at a bishop's banquet in Ireland by a lordly Anglican bishop who knew little of America and still less of the Baptists. Nearly all present at the banquet were Episcopal bishops except Truett, who decided not to be outdone in ecclesiastical rank. He was on solid ground in this, for he knew that according to the New Testament, every Baptist pastor is a bishop, for the word "bishop" means literally a shepherd of souls. Truett sat at the head table, on the right hand of the entertaining bishop.

"Since I'm not well acquainted in your country, pray, may

I ask what you are?" the host politely questioned.

"I am a Baptist," said Truett simply.

"But of course you are a bishop, are you not?" asked the Anglican dignitary.

"Oh, yes," replied Truett. "I am bishop of the First Baptist Church of Dallas, Texas."

"Oh, you then are the bishop of Dallas," announced the host.

"No," said Truett, "I am the bishop of the First Baptist Church of Dallas."

Much confused, the Anglican bishop persisted: "Oh, indeed. Somehow I had not realized that Baptists had bishops. Do you have many bishops in your Baptist denomination?"

"Yes," said Truett, with a twinkle in his eye. "I would say we have over ten thousand bishops."

"How extraordinary, perfectly amazing, upon my word," muttered the bishop in a haze of confusion. Perhaps because he realized that his leg was being pulled, he turned quickly to another subject.

The commanding figure of Dr. Truett at the congress of the Baptist World Alliance in Atlanta, Ga., where he presided over the sixty thousand delegates gathered in the ball park was not unlike that of a truly great bishop. Nearly six feet tall, of determined mien, strong willed, flashing blue-gray eyes, well proportioned, erect in stature, confident in bearing, his strong voice brought hushed attention and a warm response from the three-score thousand. Intuitively, the vast throng sensed that here was a splendid example not only of dedicated Christian manhood, but also of a tried and true preacher. His sincere self-giving in the service of Christ inspired their trust and evoked their admiration.

Beyond his vast preaching ministry, Dr. Truett gave help and encouragement to thousands of ministers in many denominations by the several books of his sermons which he prepared for publication. Many a pastor across the land was enheartened by the powerful, evangelistic spirit which surged through even his printed sermons, and thereby found a new effectiveness in his own preaching.

For years, he endured a little-known secret pain somewhat

135

like Paul's "thorn in the flesh," the messenger of Satan to buffet him. A much self-publicized preacher seemed to have an obsession to attack Dr. Truett publicly and privately on every occasion. A very close friend of Dr. Truett told me that this pulpiteer would make a point of finding out where and when Dr. Truett would be preaching. He would then have a telegram bitterly denouncing him handed to Dr. Truett just before he stepped upon the platform to preach. Though only his most intimate friends knew of it, Dr. Truett never preached on any important occasion without being hounded by this unscrupulous preacher, with his poisonous telegrams and letters of attack, all seeking to irritate, to unnerve, to anger, and to destroy Dr. Truett's well-known composure. But in all the years, he never once replied to the offender nor told anyone but his most intimate friends of this ordeal which he continually suffered.

When Dr. Truett was called to the higher service in the Temple above, the whole Southland rose irrespective of denominations to bow in thanksgiving for the life of a truly great man. In his passing not only Southern Baptists but Baptists the world over lost a friend, a lovable brother, and a preacher of the gospel whom they were proud to call their fellow Baptist — George W. Truett.

CHAPTER 16

JOHANN GERHARD ONCKEN

The Never-to-Be-Forgotten Pastor

ON THE MANTLE in the front room of a house with pointed roof in Varel, Germany, there was a picture of a young man. Five-year-old Johann looked at this picture and said to his grandmother, "Where is my daddy?"

Johann's grandmother answered: "Your daddy loved freedom and was not willing to be a slave to that wicked man, Napoleon, who invaded our beloved fatherland. With other patriotic young men, he fled across the sea to England."

"I want to see him!" cried Johann, jumping up and down for emphasis. The old lady, with one hand pressed the lad to her heart, and with her other hand wiped a tear from her eye. "Hush, hush, Johann," she said. "Your father has gone to be with God. I'm afraid you will never see him on this earth."

The church bells of Varel, Germany, were clanging loudly that Sunday morning. "I too want to go to England," sobbed Johann. "Perhaps some day you will," comforted his grandmother, "but now you must shine your shoes, for our good neighbor, 'Holy Tailor,' is coming to take you to the Lutheran Church and you must be ready."

A few years later, when Johann had become a bigger boy, a pious merchant from Scotland called on business one day at the grandmother's house. As he looked at the attractive boy he said: "I will make a man out of this lad. He needs a father and I will be like a father to him." Johann was now an upstanding lad of fourteen years. He recently had been

137

confirmed in the Lutheran Church where he had been christened as a baby. In those days of the early 1800's it was not unusual for a boy of his age to be apprenticed to some tradesman.

"Have you a Bible, my lad?" was the first question the Scotsman asked, once it had been decided that Johann was to go to Scotland with him. The merchant was shocked by Johann's reply, "No, I don't have a Bible, but I've been confirmed." To this merchant it seemed unthinkable that a Christian should not have a Bible, and he set out immediately to remedy this. He took the boy at once to a bookstore and bought him a Bible. This simple act made a deep impression on Johann, who prized his Bible dearly and later became a Baptist through studying the Bible for himself.

In 1819, Johann left Scotland for England. As he rode on the top of a London-bound bus, he said with inner satisfaction, "I'm going to England where my father went." Just then the bus gave a violent lurch, and Johann was thrown to the street where he lay bleeding from his mouth and nose. This sudden encounter with near-death prepared the nineteen-year-old youth for a sensitive response to the prayers of the London family with whom he stayed. The members of this household prayed audibly for his conversion. After a sermon in the Methodist Church, Johann really accepted Christ as Savior and Lord and made full and unreserved surrender of himself to Christ.

The zeal of Johann's conversion caused his missionary career to begin on that very same day. He was allowed a shilling a day for his dinner. This amount he now split, spending only two pennies for food and with what he saved out of his meager food allowance he bought tracts for distribution. Afterward, he wrote: "From that day I became a witness, albeit a weak one, of God's love to sinners and of his all-powerful grace." This zeal was soon to flame up into towering missionary activity which would earn for him the title, "Father of Continental Baptists," because he was the first to light the torch of the Baptist faith on the continent of Europe.

138 Burning with enthusiasm to preach the gospel, and with

Bible in hand, Johann Oncken, in 1823, came to Hamburg, Germany, as a missionary of the British Continental Society. Because of the opposition of the officers of the state church, he had to do his preaching in the cellars, the garrets, and the alleys of that city. Everywhere he went, he made it a point to distribute Bibles. Once, when he sent to the supply depot for more Bibles, the Lutheran minister in charge said to Oncken's messenger: "What becomes of all these Bibles? Does the man eat them? He shall have no more." So Oncken himself went to the depot to get the Bibles. There he was greeted with this outburst of temper: "So, *you* are the man that preaches in the cellars, garrets, and everywhere! Your cursed preaching! Whoever told you to preach?"

Johann Gerhard Oncken

Oncken replied with spirit, "The Lord Jesus Christ has commanded me to preach!" The minister sprang to his feet and said savagely, "The devil has commanded you."

Eventually Oncken's preaching rights were curbed and denied, and he then saw that more than ever he must resort to the power of the printed word of the gospel and to the distribution of Bibles. In 1828 he became an agent for the Edinburgh Bible Society, and in his lifetime he printed and distributed over two million copies of the Bible. He opened a bookshop in his home and established a printing shop and a successful publishing business still known among Baptists in Germany as the Oncken Press. Though it was destroyed by bombs from American airplanes during World War II, the publishing business has now been rebuilt and the Oncken Press is again flourishing.

When the first baby arrived in his home, Oncken, because of his independent Bible study, began to worry as to whether or not it was biblical to have the infant christened. Finally, he saw that there was no warrant in the Scriptures for infant baptism, and he accepted the New Testament concept of believer's baptism by immersion, as Jesus had been baptized. But (imagine it!) there was not a Baptist minister in all the great land of Germany by whom Oncken could be baptized! After his decision, he had to wait five years before he could find a Baptist minister who could baptize him.

Fortunately, when Oncken was thirty-four years old, on

139

April 22, 1834, Professor Barnas Sears, of Hamilton Literary and Theological Institution in the United States, who was studying in Europe at the time, responded to Oncken's heart's desire and offered his services for a midnight baptism in the river Elbe. By this time, there were six other persons who wanted to be baptized. They had to come secretly by night to the chosen spot on the river, for they risked having their goods seized by the officers and even being sent to prison. In a boat that was waiting for them at the riverside, they were quietly rowed to a lonely, secluded island. There were no lights except the silent stars, but "although externally all was dark, within us was light," said Oncken. Afterward he declared that when he walked the streets of Hamburg, it was "as if everybody must know that I had put on Christ by baptism."

Now began a more violent persecution. The aim of it was to stop Oncken's work by either bribery or persecution. At first he was offered the alluring gift of a free passage to the United States for himself and the members of his family, if only he would get out of Germany and stay far away. This he refused.

Because he refused, the expected happened; he was thrown into the Winserbaum State Prison in Hamburg. This prison, like John Bunyan's, stood close beside a bridge. One of Oncken's earliest converts, a scholarly Jew and son of a rabbi, Köbner, by name, was imprisoned in a cell located just above Oncken's. When Köbner began to sing a hymn, Oncken recognized his voice and together they joined their voices in praising God in the dank prison. Some of Oncken's church congregation gathered on the bridge beside the prison to wave to him and to give him good cheer. But they were soon scattered by the police and dared not meet again, except secretly in little groups, on account of the nearness of the ever-lurking police.

Oncken's prison cell was dark and clammy. The prison was an unsanitary place, washed on two sides by a stream of sewage which filled the air with an unwholesome stench. Consequently, Oncken caught a disease which caused him lifelong suffering. But that he kept a brave and cheerful heart may be understood from what he wrote in his prison diary: "As soon as my warden had gone, I fell on my knees blessing and praising the Savior who counted me worthy to suffer imprisonment for his name's sake. I felt well and happy and prayed for the conversion of my persecutors." He tried to persuade his jailer to become a Christian.

Oncken suffered numerous imprisonments and seemed to live under the threat of sudden arrest. One day when he was with a few friends in a public garden on the shore of the river Elbe, an unknown woman approached him and whispered in his ear, "Dragoons are at the garden park gate waiting to take you prisoner as you leave." With the fleet feet of a deer, Oncken leaped over a hedge, dashed forward, and bounded down a hill to the edge of the river. There he spied a friend with a boat. "You are sent of the Lord to help me escape to Hamburg," cried Oncken, jumping into the boat, which sped him away to safety. On many other occasions Oncken had to escape from the traps his enemies set for him.

Meanwhile, the work of the Baptists advanced as it always has done under persecution. The First Baptist Church, which had been established in Hamburg, in 1834, with only seven members, had by this time grown to a congregation of several hundred, and had come into the ownership of a four-story building which had once been a warehouse.

In this same year, Oncken was appointed by the American Baptists as their organizing missionary in Germany and Europe. Baptists of America continued to help Oncken through many years. Perhaps he could not have carried on so successfully without the great help he received from the Baptists in America. Little did American Baptists realize, however, the many ways in which Oncken would repay them. To mention only one, Oncken baptized the grandfather of Dr. Herbert Gezork. Dr. Gezork became one of the most honored presidents of the American Baptist Convention and he continues to serve notably as the president of Andover Newton Theological School, American Baptists' oldest theological seminary.

The persecution of Baptists in Hamburg was halted

temporarily by a most disastrous fire which, in 1842, left one third of the city in ruins. Pastor Oncken. without delay, opened three stories of the Baptist Church building to provide a place of refuge for the homeless. For a time after this evidence of kindness, the people of Hamburg had less heart for persecuting the Baptists.

Nevertheless, even this was forgotten, and before persecution finally ended Oncken was twice more imprisoned at Winserbaum. It was not until 1860 that a law was passed that gave full freedom to all denominations.

Much of the success of Oncken's work was due to his persistence in following the policy symbolized by his watchword, "Every Baptist a Missionary." By his own zealous example, he fired his converts to witness for Christ immediately and everywhere.

Like Paul, Oncken was a great traveler; he visited widely scattered groups of Baptist believers and established churches all over Germany. By 1849 there were enough Baptist churches in four associations to form the "Union of the Associated Churches of Baptized Christians in Germany and Denmark." Possessed of a statesman's view, Oncken always insisted on the need for a school to train ministers and on a vigorous Baptist publishing enterprise. He was a great believer in the power of the printed word. In 1880, as a result of his efforts, the Baptists finally established the Hamburg Theological Seminary.

Oncken's missionary zeal could not be confined, however, to Germany. He carried his work into Denmark where, in 1839, he founded the First Baptist Church in Copenhagen; and into the Netherlands where he founded a Baptist church in 1846. In 1847 he baptized F. O. Nilsson, a founder of the Baptist work in Sweden. So, too, Poland and Russia engaged his interest.

When he was seventy years of age, Oncken undertook a long and strenuous missionary journey into Russia. He traveled in a rough wagon without springs or seat, jolting over roads which caused "his knees and mouth very nearly to meet." By night he slept in the wagon on a pile of straw. Often he could find little to eat. Sometimes, as in the steppes, he had to travel by night to avoid the fearful heat.

Finally he came to Odessa in a state of nervous exhaustion. Yet he pushed on into Romania and Bulgaria. He wrote of his journey over the Carpathian Mountains: "A journey of forty-eight hours over rock and stone, through bogs and morasses, across rivers and over pathless tracts of country . . . to my no small horror, I heard of the dangers as soon as I had gotten into the wagon, both as to the impossible roads and the frequent attacks of banditti. Not a pleasant introduction to a long journey, but extremity leads to prayer."

Oncken made converts wherever he went. He baptized them and strengthened and inspired the believers at scores of places. At last he returned to his homeland of Germany, a tired old man, but still not lacking in vigor or in vision.

It was a great day for Oncken when he dedicated the new First Baptist Church in Hamburg, a beautiful building seating a congregation of 1,400 persons. Americans and Britishers had contributed funds to help make possible the erection of this church edifice. The occasion was made significant by the presence of Charles Haddon Spurgeon, who preached the dedication sermon on April 17, 1867. It was Mr. Spurgeon who afterward told the young preachers of Germany, "Preach not only so people can understand, but so that they cannot misunderstand even if they wish."

When Oncken neared eighty years of age and was able to look back over his years of strenuous and tireless missionary service, he seemed to realize that he was nearing the end of his career. "My health is gone," he wrote, "and my bodily sufferings are such that I can only wish to depart and see my Lord and Savior in all his glory." His desire was fulfilled, for when he was eighty-four years old he breathed his last. So was terminated his earthly mission. His church placed a monument by his grave. The inscription on it states that it had been erected by the church "in memory of their never-to-be-forgotten pastor."

CHAPTER 17

WALTER RAUSCHENBUSCH

Prophet of Social Justice

"Is IT TRUE THAT YOU are a minister's son?" asked a theological student of his professor of church history at the close of a class session.

The deaf teacher, who read lips, smiled broadly, revealing a fine set of teeth shining through his red beard. "Yes, I'm not only a minister's son, but I'm sixth in a line of succession of ministers. Putting it in another way, my father, who was a minister, was also the son, the grandson, the great-grandson, and the great-great-grandson of a minister."

Greatly beloved of his students at the Rochester Theological Seminary, the professor, in the year 1902, was still in the vigor of his ministry. Even his scholarly German background and unique ministerial family heritage, however, had not yet disclosed the full measure of the fame that thenceforth would always be attached to the name, Walter Rauschenbusch.

"Yes," he continued intimately, as a coterie of students gathered about his desk in the classroom, "now that you ask, I was born here in Rochester just seven years after my father and mother emigrated to this country. My father was originally a Lutheran. He became a Baptist not by birth but by conviction. You see, he came here as a Baptist missionary to the many German immigrants who were pouring into the United States. Soon his scholarly attainments led this seminary to call him to teach in its German Department."

The expression on the faces of the circling students showed 145 that they were eager to hear more. "Although I was only five years of age at the time, I can recall the shock to my family and to the entire community, on that fatal April 15, 1865, upon hearing the news of the assassination of Abraham Lincoln. I well remember helping my father hang a heavy crape on the front door of our home, as tears fell from his eyes for our dead President."

"You have a vivid memory of your boyhood experiences," remarked a student.

"Yes, indeed," said Rauschenbusch. "I can recall how my mother took me as a child to Germany, where I went to school in Barmen for three years. I think also I shall never forget working each summer on a farm in Lycoming County, Pennsylvania. That was while I was a student attending the Academy. I tried to earn some money by working summers on this farm. In those days we worked from sunup, around 4:30 A.M., to sundown, around 8:00 P.M. A long, long day. Now, how much do you suppose I earned? Well, I received the munificent salary of twenty-five cents a day. Oh, yes, and I forgot to mention, I also earned something to eat, but not much!"

One of the students standing close by said, "Well, Professor, that would average about two cents an hour." "You're just about right," answered his teacher, "and you will understand why I, because of that experience, long ago decided that I would always fight against oppressive hours of labor."

The bell rang for the next class. Reluctantly the students dispersed.

Born on October 4, 1861, Walter Rauschenbusch had the first great decisive hours of his career when he was aged seventeen. Facing the problems of growing out of boyhood into manhood, he implored in fervent prayers the help of God, his heavenly Father. He experienced a deep, tender, and mysterious response from God, which, he declared, influenced his soul down to its depths. "His life's direction was determined," says one of his biographers, "by this religious experience, this conversion."

About this time also he decided to enter the ministry. In
146   heroic spirit, after he had completed the studies which took

him to Germany to the University of Berlin and through the Theological Seminary at Rochester, he offered himself for foreign missionary service. Failing of appointment to India, he plunged into the jungle of Hell's Kitchen in New York City, where he became pastor of the small and poor congregation of the Second German Baptist Church.

For eleven years he served there as pastor. His church was located on the edge of New York's notorious slums. In that tough tenement neighborhood he ministered to life in the raw. In seeking to serve his people, he grappled at first hand with such problems of the underprivileged as malnutrition, destitution, overcrowded tenements, unemployment, sickness without proper medical care, the indignities of the exploitation of the poor, and the crime-breeding streets of the slums. With self-sacrificing spirit, and on a salary of only six hundred dollars a year after deducting his rent, Walter Rauschenbusch labored with prophetic zeal. He joined hands with Jacob Riis to build playgrounds for children, to work for decent housing, and to fight corruption in politics. Wherever he uncovered injustices and social evil, his soul was fired with hot indignation. Inevitably, by his ministry in the slums, he gained profound insights into social problems.

Out of those eleven years, he was led by the circumstances of his ministry and the providence of God to what amounted to a second conversion experience. In it he gained a radically new outlook on the full meaning of the gospel and the kingdom of God. From this time forward, his life was marked by an even greater social passion. "It did not come from the church," he confessed. (In his day, great leaders of the church were saying, "It is not the mission of the church to abolish physical misery.") "It came from the outside," said Rauschenbusch. "It came through personal contact with poverty. When I saw how men toiled all their lifelong, hard, toilsome lives, and at the end had almost nothing to show for it, how strong men begged for work and could not get it; how little children died — oh, the children's funerals! They gripped my heart."

From this experience he went on to a deeper study of the Bible. As a result of it, he discovered a new viewpoint. He 147 came to see that there was no conflict "between a gospel for the individual and a gospel big enough to redeem the whole social system." He began to emphasize the fact that whereas "our inherited Christian faith dealt with individuals, our present task deals with society."

The fierce energies he expended in service to the poor so weakened his strength, however, that in 1888 he was stricken with a severe attack of the grippe. Suffering a relapse, the ravages of the fever left him with deafness — a malady from which he suffered throughout the last thirty years of his life. This handicap, with its attendant sense of isolation, brought to him, as to Thomas A. Edison, a sense of loneliness; but by shutting out much human noise and distraction, it undoubtedly quickened his spiritual perception and gave him silence in which to think deeply and to write powerfully.

Fortunately, in 1897, the Rochester Seminary, where his father had taught for thirty years, now called Walter Rauschenbusch, the son, to a chair in the German Department. His deafness placed no limitation on his ability as a lecturer, neither did it lower his effectiveness as a professor. In 1902, he was transferred to the English Department of the Seminary, which is now known as the Colgate Rochester Divinity School. From the Seminary chair, where he served for twenty-one years, he found a new way to disseminate his ideas. His position as a professor gave him a platform for the expression of his concern for the social interpretation of the gospel.

In awakening the complacent church to the dire social problems of the day, Rauschenbusch often for his illustrations had recourse to homely metaphors drawn from his own rugged experiences. For example, in dealing with the problem of excessive wealth he remembered those hot summer days when he worked on the farm. Attacking the evil of the concentration of wealth in the hands of a few, he wrote: "Wealth is to a nation what manure is to a farm. If the farmer spreads it evenly over the soil it will enrich the whole. If he should leave it in heaps, the land would be impoverished and under the rich heaps the vegetation would be killed."

Dr. Rauschenbusch now began to put his ideas into books that commanded national attention. He pleaded that religion should take its proper and momentous part in the solving of the social crises of the times. He brought his biblical studies to bear upon the relation of social problems to the kingdom of God. His great book, *Christianity and the Social Crisis,* published in 1907, hit the reading public just at the time when Americans were beginning to have an uneasy conscience about a number of social problems.

Strenuous Theodore Roosevelt, trust buster, wielder of the Big Stick, and advocate of conservation, was attacking "malefactors of great wealth." Christian leaders were beginning to be upset by the injustice of sweatshops, the long hours of forced labor of children in factories, and the spread of diseases in crowded slums. A whiff of social reform could be felt in the breeze sweeping across the country, and Dr. Rauschenbusch's book came as a powerful wind which blew away the church's complacency. His work strengthened the labor movement at a time when labor unions were not strong, but were slowly growing in the face of stiff opposition. Many church men espoused "the social gospel." Rauschenbusch predicted that the social forces in the United States presented "an irrepressible conflict" in which religion had to play a decisive part. He said in his book, "All the characteristic conditions of American life will henceforth combine to make the social struggle here more intense than anywhere else. The vastness and the free sweep of our concentrated wealth on the one side, the independence, intelligence, moral vigor, and political power of the common people on the other side, promise a long-drawn grapple of contesting forces. . . ."

Books now began to flow from this social prophet's pen. *For God and the People: Prayers of the Social Awakening* appeared in 1910 and is still widely used. In 1912 he published *Christianizing the Social Order.* His last great book, *A Theology for the Social Gospel,* was published in 1917. It reflected his long experience and matured thinking. Meanwhile he continued to play a conspicuous part in the American scene. By means of his lectures, writings, preaching, 149 teaching, and counsel, he prodded the American conscience toward social reform.

Never a lover of war and always abhorring bloodshed, his spirit was too sensitive to give aid to the destructive forces which in 1914 engulfed the world with the outbreak of the First World War. He was too wise to respond to much of the false propaganda which stirred up the peace-loving American people to go to war against Germany. Unfortunately his silence, together with his German background, made him a victim of bitter criticism by excited patriots who were seeing German spies behind every bush on the lawn. He felt himself under suspicion and suffered the disillusionment and pain which come to a sensitive spirit who finds himself misunderstood. Holding that "war is the most sinful thing there is," Rauschenbusch wore crape on the lapel of his coat when the war began, with the intention of keeping it there until the war was over.

In 1918 his body was wracked by a fatally progressive cancer. As he felt death approaching, he wrote to a friend, "Since 1914 the world is full of hate and I cannot expect to be happy again in my lifetime." When his bodily strength was much weakened, he whispered to Dr. Clarence A. Barbour, the president of the Seminary: "I am not sorry to be leaving a world where there is so much hate and to be going to a country where there will be so much love."

Dr. Robert G. Torbet has beautifully said, "On July 25, 1918, a tall, slender man, his red beard streaked with gray, his body cancered, his spirit broken by the tragedy of world conflict, 'stepped through the little "Postern Gate" to be with God.' "

CHAPTER 18

HELEN BARRETT MONTGOMERY

The Most Distinguished Woman Among Baptists

"LIFE SEEMED SO GRAND and beautiful . . . ," Helen Barrett wrote to her "little sister" in a burst of joy following upon her engagement. The happy and fortunate man was William A. Montgomery, a Philadelphia businessman.

What Helen wrote, to give it more fully, was: "Life seemed so grand and beautiful *as we rose from our knees*." It was a *kneeling* engagement, all right; only in this case, instead of the man kneeling in front of the woman, the man and the woman knelt together before the all-highest God. Amazing lovers, Helen and William had knelt in prayer in a double dedication to each other and to the making of God's service pre-eminent in their lives.

This brilliant young woman had been baptized and had joined the church at the age of fifteen. Her spirit is further revealed in the letter from which the above sentence has been quoted. "I am anxious," she wrote, "that my whole life may be given without reserve to God's service. . . . Before he [Will] went away, he knelt with me and together we consecrated our lives to God's work in the world, promising to make this work our first thought. . . . Life seemed so grand and beautiful as we rose from our knees."

Indeed, her life would be "grand," for she would be the first woman in America ever to be made the official head of a great denomination. She became, in later years, the first president of what is now the American Baptist Convention. So too, her life would be "beautiful," for she would be the first and only woman ever to translate the New Testament from the original Greek into English and to have her translation published and widely circulated.

Nevertheless, married life would bring to Mrs. Helen Barrett Montgomery its testing and trials. They would need all the strength they could summon to keep from breaking their engagement promise to put God's work first in their lives. The severest trial came after William had become a successful businessman, and when he and Helen were living in a comfortable home in Rochester, N. Y.

It was just because Mr. Montgomery was such a keen and adventurous businessman that the trouble began. He agreed with a young inventor that there ought to be a better way to start an automobile than to stand in front of the car in the face of danger and turn an awkward crank.

"Did you hear that John Cousins broke his wrist yesterday morning while trying to crank his car when it was so awfully cold?" Helen inquired of her husband as she put up the telephone receiver.

"No, but worse yet, the morning paper reports that Harold White forgot to put on the emergency brake before he began to crank his car; the engine started suddenly and his car ran over him. He's now on the danger list in the hospital." Mr. Montgomery was greatly disturbed. "You know, my dear," he continued, "there is a young inventor who has a device that could correct this, if only we could perfect it and put it on the market."

No sooner had he said this than the doorbell rang. Mr. Montgomery opened the door to a bright young man who entered smiling.

"Helen," Mr. Montgomery said, "this is the young inventor friend of mine of whom I was speaking. He is working on a device that will be a self-starter for automobiles. If it proves successful, it will do away with all these broken wrists and arms and run-over bodies that we were talking about. It will no longer be necessary for a man to stand in front of his car in order to crank it. I'm going to back this young man financially, even though it may cost me heavily."

152

"Thank you, Mr. Montgomery," bowed the young man.

"I'm sure I'm going to find the answer someday, but I'm sorry to tell you that the model I've been working on has failed again. I believe I now have a better idea of how this can be made to work, but it will take a few thousand dollars more to create and perfect this invention for use."

And so it was that Mr. Montgomery kept pouring out money while backing this young inventor. He had given his word, and he had faith both in the inventor and in the possibility of a successful invention.

Nevertheless, day by day, Mr. Montgomery's financial resources shrank steadily. He soon was down to almost his last dollar. He could not conceal his financial difficulties from his wife.

"How is it that you are getting the dinner tonight and serving the meals? Where is the maid?" asked Mr. Montgomery.

"Oh," said his wife, assuming a jaunty air, "I let the maid go, for I can do my own housework. We can't afford keeping a maid, if you are to go ahead with your invention."

"Bless you, my dear Helen," said her husband. "But really, I hate to see you making a slave of yourself in this big house."

"Don't worry," she said. "We prayed together and we stay together."

Somehow the pastor of the church of which they were members (the Lake Avenue Baptist Church in Rochester, N. Y.) became aware of what was happening. One day he met Mr. Montgomery on the street.

"You pledged very heavily to our church, Mr. Montgomery," said the pastor. "I believe that even if you were to cut your pledge down a bit, you would still be on record as the most generous giver in our membership. Why don't you do it?"

"Oh, no, no, pastor," said Mr. Montgomery with strong emphasis. "I'll never cut my pledge to the church, no matter what comes."

A few months later at breakfast, Mr. Montgomery said to his wife, "Well, I may as well be honest with you. I'm practically on the rocks financially and I've a good mind to give

Helen Barrett Montgomery

153

up this adventure. I will have to, unless I can get hold of some money quickly."

"No," said Helen. "You have a good idea and you must not give up. I know a way by which I can get you some money by tomorrow. Don't ask me how, but I just believe that I can do it."

That night, when Mr. Montgomery came home and dropped wearily into a chair, he saw that something was missing from the living room.

"What's become of the piano?" he asked. "Oh, you must have sold it to get the quick money you were talking about. I can never endure this. We are so near to success with the invention that I would like to hold on, but this is too much of a sacrifice for you. For you, who loves music so much! I'd better give up."

Putting an arm around her husband, Helen said: "I got an amazingly good price for the piano and here is the money I promised you. Now take it and be happy about it, for I am. I believe in you and you believe in the invention."

The next day when the pastor was making his afternoon calls, one of his parishioners asked him if he had heard that friends had seen piano movers taking the concert grand piano away from the Montgomery home. Someone had seen Helen holding the door open for the movers and wiping a tear from her eye with the corner of her white lace-edged apron.

The pastor broke off his calls at the homes in the neighborhood and slipped down to Mr. Montgomery's office.

"Mr. Montgomery, as your pastor, you must permit me to talk with you quite confidentially. I know that you are in deep waters financially. I've also learned of the sacrifice of Mrs. Montgomery in selling her piano. I know what this means to her with her love of beautiful music. Now, some of us feel that perhaps you've pledged too heavily to the church and I'm here to suggest that you reduce your pledge by at least one-half. Even then the gift that remains will be very generous."

"Thank you, pastor, for your concern, but my answer is no. My church pledge is the last thing in the world I shall ever cut. Oh, the time may come when I cannot raise enough dollars to pay for it, but I shall not cut it, I can assure you of that."

The pastor closed the office door behind him. As he went down the hall of the office building, he murmured to himself: "This man is genuinely sincere. He really believes, deep in his soul, in being a faithful steward of God. Would that I had more laymen like him! May God reward his loyalty and steadfastness."

And God did. The invention was a success. Soon it was a *great* success. The automobile self-starter became widely used, and finally, the crank was everywhere discontinued. With increasing business success, Mr. Montgomery, with great liberality, increased his gifts to the church.

"You stood by me, sweetheart," Mr. Montgomery said one night when he gave Helen a generous check.

"I promised, didn't I, when we knelt together at the time of our engagement and life became so grand and so beautiful?"

Now that Mr. and Mrs. Montgomery were once more in comfortable circumstances, Mrs. Montgomery gave rein to her love of the beautiful as she had discovered it in the Greek language. She had studied Greek at Wellesley College in the days when Alice E. Freeman (Palmer) was president. In this, she was following in the tradition of her father, who had been at one time a teacher of Latin and Greek. "I think Greek is very beautiful," she often said to her friends.

Now, her love of Greek was about to be put to an important use. The American Baptist Publication Society, to mark the first hundred years of its history, wanted to publish a significant book which would exemplify one of its great objectives, that of circulating the Scriptures. Helen Barrett Montgomery had translated into English, out of the original Greek, the entire New Testament. This was just the book the American Baptist Publication Society was seeking. It was published as the Centenary Translation.

While her work was scholarly, it was also done in the words of everyday life in accordance with the original character of the New Testament Greek. The publication of her

translation met with instant acclaim, and it has continued to be so appealing that already her translation has had sixteen printings. It now bears the title, *The New Testament in Modern English.*

In this work, she made it her aim: "To offer a translation in the language of everyday life. . . . To make a translation chiefly designed for the ordinary reader and intended to remove the veil that a literary or formal translation inevitably puts between the reader of only average education and the meaning of the text."

It was her wish "to stimulate the daily reading of the Gospels" through a low-priced translation, "in a form easy to be carried in the pocket or in a handbag." She records that the arduous years of scholarly labor were a "work of love . . . years of happy work" given "in deep humility." With her translation she provided topical headlines to make the reading more orderly and exciting.

As she sent the last pages of her manuscript to the American Baptist Publication Society, she pondered why she had been so happily and naturally driven to this hard work of translating the entire New Testament. Somehow her mind recalled her childhood impressions when she had heard how her grandfather Barrett each night used to have his eight children stand in line for Bible instruction and family prayers. One of those eight had been her own father, Adoniram Judson Barrett. Her grandmother's sincere piety also had fascinated her as a child and she remembered well how "Grandmother Barrett . . . used to retreat to a small house outside for her daily season of prayer. I used to steal after her and stand outside the closed door where I could listen to her dear voice as she prayed for each of her family in turn."

Yes, the grandparents had had a share in this translation, she agreed within herself, and now they would be happy with the result.

And why, pray, had they named her father Adoniram Judson, if they had not had also a great missionary passion?

So very naturally, growing out of her family traditions, she too came to have an ardent interest in foreign missions.

The Baptist women saw in her a leader of unusual abilities. For ten years, 1914 to 1924, she served with great distinction as president of the Woman's American Baptist Foreign Mission Society.

This presidency was no empty office. Mrs. Montgomery stirred the Christian women of America of all denominations to help found and support the Seven Colleges for the Women of Asia. As she and Mrs. Henry W. Peabody (twin souls with a passionate concern for the kingdom of Christ) toured the mission lands, they were appalled by the lack of Christian reading material for the new converts and for the members of the young Christian churches. In consequence, they were led to found a strategically important organization known as the Committee on World Christian Literature. Mrs. Montgomery gave the initial $25,000 to start this important work. She knew full well that the new mission churches could not grow to stability and strong leadership without the undergirding of Christian literature for readers in their own tongues.

American Baptists have come to recognize that in Helen Barrett Montgomery, M.A., D.H.L., LL.D., (Brown, Dennison, and Franklin gave her honorary degrees) they had their most distinguished woman.

At her death, confirming her love of the kingdom of God, she bequeathed nearly one-half million dollars to hospitals, colleges, missions, and various Christian causes.

Scholarly, she never lost the human touch; president of a large denomination, she never forgot the local church; as a wife, she never forsook her husband when he needed her sacrifices; energetic, she encompassed the world to advance Christian missions; possessed of wealth, she gave it all away in the service of Christ.

But perhaps her best right to enduring remembrance is her beautiful translation of the New Testament dedicated "To the supreme task of circulating the Scriptures."

Indeed, her memory is "so grand and beautiful"!

CHAPTER 19

BAPTIST HYMN WRITERS

WHEN YOU HOLD your hymnbook in church and join with others in singing, you ought to know that the idea of singing hymns rather than singing only psalms first took shape in the musical soul and mind of a Baptist pastor in England.

It was Benjamin Keach who started the practice of congregational hymn-singing in English-speaking churches. Before his day, congregations droned out "The Psalms of David" in unexciting tunes sung in a slow tempo. Keach, a prolific writer, decided to do something about this. Accordingly he produced popular gospel hymns for his church congregation to sing. In 1691 he published a book of over three hundred hymns, called *Spiritual Melody*.

You see, when Baptists were under persecution, printed words could be dangerous to them, so they developed a technique of using verses as an aid to memory. They discovered that rhymed instruction was easy for the illiterate people in their churches to remember. Rather naturally, this practice grew into the plan of fitting their verses of rhymed doctrines to musical accompaniments. Thomas Smith, for example, wrote for his church a total of one thousand, one hundred hymns which contained a complete system of doctrine, experience, and practice.

But it was Benjamin Keach who really started the plan of congregational singing. He was attacked for this supposedly heretical innovation — "carnal formalities," they called it — and many members left his church because he insisted on encouraging the singing of hymns by the whole congregation. His idea caught fire, however, and though there was fierce doctrinal controversy, eventually all over the land people sang hymns in the churches with joy and thanksgiving.

Not only did Keach's writing get him into trouble with other church people, but also the government wanted to stop him from writing Baptist doctrine for children. He wrote a primer for children in which he taught Baptist beliefs. For this, the constables came one day to his home and arrested him.

Standing as a prisoner in the court at Aylesbury, on October 9, 1664, he held himself with dignity while Chief Justice Hyde roared at him: "Benjamin Keach, you are here convicted of writing and publishing a seditious and scandalous book; you shall go to prison for a fortnight and the next Saturday stand in a pillory for two hours from eleven o'clock until one with a paper upon your head with this inscription: 'for writing and printing and publishing a schismatical book entitled, *The Child Instructor* or *A New and Easy Primer*,' and the next Thursday to stand in the same manner and for that same time in the market of Winslow, and there your book shall openly be burnt before your face by the common hangman in disgrace of you and your doctrine, and you shall forfeit to the king's majesty the sum of twenty pounds."

However, in spite of the fact that Keach saw his books burned and that he suffered imprisonment, he continued to write the happy songs of Zion and to print his books for the children whom he loved. Through all the years since, Baptists have continued to write hymns, and some of the best-loved hymns were written by our Baptist fathers.

When at the close of the Lord's Supper many congregations sing, "Blest Be the Tie that Binds Our Hearts in Christian Love," they are singing a hymn written by John Fawcett, pastor of the Baptist Church at Wainsgate, England. He was a good and true pastor whom his people came to love very dearly.

In 1772, Fawcett received a call to go to a famous church
160 in London and felt led to accept the call. After his goods

were packed and he was ready to move to the big city, his people came around him with their farewells. So great was their weeping that his heart melted as he realized their great affection for him. Neither he nor his wife could endure the sadness expressed by these people as they thought of losing their pastor. Finally, under tense emotion, he said: "Well, I shall stay here. You may help me unpack my things, and we shall live for the Lord lovingly together."

After this moving experience he wrote the beautiful lines:

> Blest be the tie that binds
> Our hearts in Christian love:
> The fellowship of kindred minds
> Is like to that above.

> When we are called to part,
> It gives us inward pain;
> But we shall still be joined in heart,
> And hope to meet again.

One of the great hymns which Americans have loved and which at one time was considered to be our national anthem, "My Country, 'Tis of Thee," was written by a Baptist pastor, Samuel Francis Smith, whose home still stands in one of the suburbs of Boston. Smith was a student in what is now Andover Newtown Theological School, where his ability to translate languages was well known. In fact, before his death at eighty-six years of age, he had mastered fifteen different languages and was about to begin the study of Russian. A traveler returning from Germany brought home many German song books and gave them to the young Smith to see whether or not some of the songs might be suitable for translation into English. In going over them Smith's eye fell upon the tune now known as "America," but which really was first chosen by the English for use with the words, "God Save the King." Under sudden inspiration, Smith reached down into the wastebasket in his seminary room, pulled out a scrap of paper, and within a half-hour's time had written the words:

> My country! 'tis of thee,
> Sweet land of liberty,
> Of thee I sing:

Land where my fathers died!
Land of the pilgrims' pride!
From every mountain side
Let freedom ring!

This hymn was first sung on the Fourth of July, 1832, in the city of Boston in the Park Street Church, located opposite Boston Common on the site which came to be known as "Brimstone Corner." It was this same Samuel Francis Smith who wrote the hymn which moved the foreign mission society to save the Lone Star Mission in India.

Many Baptists fervently sing the hymn written by John Henry Gilmore, entitled "He Leadeth Me":

He leadeth me: O blessed thought!
O words with heavenly comfort fraught!
Whate'er I do, where'er I be,
Still 'tis God's hand that leadeth me.

Dr. Gilmore had just finished conducting a prayer meeting in the First Baptist Church in Philadelphia where he had spoken on the Twenty-third Psalm. When he returned to the house where he was a guest, the discussion of God's guidance continued. Subsequently he wrote: "During the conversation the blessedness of God's leadership so settled upon me that I took up my pencil and wrote the hymn just as it stands today — handed it to my wife and thought no more about it. She sent it without my knowledge to the *Watchman and Reflector*." The hymn has remained a very popular one and has brought blessing to many thousands. Dr. Gilmore was the son of the governor of New Hampshire. He was a graduate of Brown University and of Newton Theological Institution. He wrote this hymn in 1862.

John Bunyan also was a hymn writer, but only one of his hymns has been given a place in our Baptist hymnbook. Strangely enough, the Anglican (Episcopal) Church which persecuted John Bunyan has now placed this hymn in its official hymnbook.

Bunyan's love of singing is reflected in what he wrote in *The Pilgrim's Progress*. "The pilgrim they laid in a large upper chamber, whose windows opened towards the rising sun. The name of the chamber was *Peace,* where he slept 'til break of day, and then he awoke and sang." The lines of the hymn are as follows:

> He who would valiant be
> 'Gainst all disaster,
> Let him in constancy
> Follow the Master.
> There's no discouragement
> Shall make him once relent
> His first avow'd intent
> To be a pilgrim.
>
> Who so beset him round
> With dismal stories,
> Do but themselves confound,
> His strength the more is.
> No foes shall stay his might,
> Tho' he with giants fight;
> He will make good his right
> To be a pilgrim.
>
> Since, Lord, thou dost defend
> Us with thy Spirit,
> We know we at the end
> Shall life inherit.
> Then fancies, flee away!
> I'll fear not what men say,
> I'll labor night and day
> To be a pilgrim.

Bunyan wrote his hymn originally for Valiant-for-truth in his *The Pilgrim's Progress*. Before it was revised by the hymnbook editors, the first stanza read:

> Who would true valour see,
> Let him come hither;
> One here will constant be,
> Come wind, come weather;
> There's no discouragement
> Shall make him once relent
> His first avow'd intent
> To be a pilgrim.

Baptists have not only contributed writers for the words of hymns, but also composers who have created the melodies.

One of the best-known Baptist American hymn composers was William H. Doane, who as a young man joined the Baptist Church in Norwich, Conn. His love of music developed at an early age, and when he was only six years old he was often called upon to sing in public. He joined the church choir at the age of ten. He played the contrabass when he was thirteen and became an organist when he was sixteen. He composed the music for such hymns as, "Rescue the Perishing," "Safe in the Arms of Jesus," "Jesus, Keep Me Near the Cross," "Pass Me Not, O Gentle Savior," "More Love to Thee, O Christ," "Take the Name of Jesus With You," and scores of others.

A Baptist hymn in which both the author of the words and the composer of the music were Baptists is the well-known "Savior, Thy Dying Love Thou Gavest Me." The author was Sylvanus D. Phelps and the composer was Robert Lowry.

Dr. Phelps was born at Suffield, Conn., and after graduation from Brown University and Yale Divinity School, he served for twenty-eight years as pastor of the First Baptist Church in New Haven. He began writing hymns during his college years and was the author of a great many poems. The hymn, "Savior, Thy Dying Love Thou Gavest Me," is a great favorite among Baptists, for it portrays the sacrifice of Christ as the atonement for sinners and suggests a grateful return to love and loyalty to Christ on the part of the redeemed. The closing verse is a prayer for undying devotion and a life of humble service to this crucified Lord.

But there also have been women among the Baptists who have been able writers of hymns. Many a person caught in temptation must be thankful to Mrs. Annie Sherwood Hawks who wrote the beautiful hymn, "I Need Thee Every Hour."

> I need thee every hour;
> Stay thou near by;
> Temptations lose their power
> When thou art nigh.

Her interest in hymn writing started when she became a member of the Hanson Place Baptist Church in Brooklyn, N. Y., where Dr. Robert Lowry, the hymn composer, was then pastor. He encouraged Mrs. Hawks in her hymn writing and he wrote the music to the words of this hymn. This hymn spontaneously sprang out of her heart while she was doing her daily housework. As she moved about in the kitchen, the dining room, and the living room, she was conscious of needing Christ's presence with her even as she engaged in routine domestic duties. The hymn promptly found wide use and has made for itself a secure place in Christian worship.

A voluminous writer of hymns and poems was Miss Anne Steele, out of whose tragic life was born the beautiful hymn:

> Father, whate'er of earthly bliss
> Thy sovereign will denies,
> Accepted at thy throne of grace,
> Let this petition rise:
>
> Give me a calm, a thankful heart,
> From every murmur free;
> The blessings of thy grace impart,
> And make me live to thee.
>
> Let the sweet hope that thou art mine
> My life and death attend;
> Thy presence through my journey shine,
> And crown my journey's end.

She was an invalid from her childhood and at times a great sufferer. "When she was twenty-one years of age, the young man to whom she was engaged to be married was drowned while in bathing, the day before the wedding was to take place. Yet, heartbroken, she did not yield to despair but made herself a ministering spirit devoting her life to deeds of love and mercy. Many of her hymns, written to lighten her own burdens, give beautiful expressions to the sweetness of her Christian character and the depth of her Christian experience."

Her journey's end was crowned as she had desired. Weeping friends gathered around her deathbed and at "the happy moment of her dismission, she closed her eyes and said with dying lips, 'I know that my Redeemer liveth.' She gently fell asleep in Jesus."

There are few Christians who have not been melted into a fresh sense of devotion by singing the beautiful hymn:

My Jesus, I love thee, I know thou art mine;
For thee all the follies of sin I resign;
My gracious Redeemer, my Savior art thou;
If ever I loved thee, my Jesus, 'tis now.

Tales of Baptist Daring

This song was written by a Baptist preacher, Dr. Adoniram Judson Gordon, who was pastor of the Clarendon Street Baptist Church, Boston. It was he who baptized in a pond at Northfield, Mass., the famous evangelist, Dwight L. Moody. Dr. Gordon also founded what is now known as the Gordon Divinity School, until recently located in Boston, and was the author of a number of books. He was once arrested for preaching the gospel on Boston Common. The words of the hymn first appeared as a poem in a Canadian periodical. Some years later, a friend of Gordon's, on returning from England, brought the poem to the Boston pastor and said, "These words would make a beautiful hymn." Dr. Gordon sat down to his piano and pecked out a simple tune which a composer helped him to complete.

A recent hymn which already is widely used in Christian churches of all denominations is the hymn by Dr. Harry Emerson Fosdick, entitled "God of Grace and God of Glory." Dr. Fosdick was born in Buffalo, N. Y., of parents who were devout Baptists and educators as well. At the age of seven, the precocious Harry determined that he would be baptized. Afterward he said that this was his first independent decision. In later years, after he had recovered from a serious nervous breakdown, he was for a long time the most famous preacher in America. His books of sermons sold widely. He built a beautiful church on Morningside Heights, New York City, modeled somewhat after a French cathedral. This church is now called the Riverside Church because it overlooks the Hudson River.

His hymn, "God of Grace and God of Glory," appeals for strength for this hour, and is peculiarly fitted to the mood and need of this time of conflict in the history of the world. Its popularity is richly deserved and possibly it will remain an even greater monument to Dr. Fosdick than the church edifice which he built.

CHAPTER 20

ANECDOTES of STURDY BAPTIST PIONEERS

Their Belief in Prayer

It was a rainy April day in Malden, Mass., when Dr. A. F. Ufford, a missionary from China, greeted me with a smile from under his huge umbrella. I was depressed over reports of mission fields closed by World War II.

"Come to luncheon with me," said Dr. Ufford.

Since it meant having luncheon in the house where Adoniram Judson was born, I accepted the invitation with alacrity.

While we were seated at the table, I asked Mrs. Ufford, "How did you happen to go to China as a missionary?" Her answer was a story of the astonishing faith of one of our Baptist pioneers.

"My Grandfather Hartwell graduated from Brown University in 1819," she began, "and offered himself to the Baptists as a missionary to Burma. He had a great desire to follow in the footsteps of Adoniram Judson. The Board accepted him, but when the physical examination took place the doctors turned him down. He had weak lungs. The doctors said that in Burma he would not survive more than six months.

"My grandfather," Mrs. Ufford continued, "was plunged into bitter despair. He had felt so certain that God had called him to go to Burma. Meanwhile he married a beautiful Christian woman. He finally worked his way out of despair by getting assurance that, though he could not go   167 himself, God would send him a son who would go as a missionary.

"When many months later a baby was coming to the Hartwell home, Grandfather, who was a man of fervent prayer life, assured his friends that the baby would be a son who would grow to be a missionary. When the baby was born, it proved to be a girl. This came as another shock to Grandfather Hartwell, but he continued to pray that God would send him a son. But the second baby also was a girl. If Grandfather had anything," said Mrs. Ufford, "he had persistency of faith. When the third child was coming, he had not a doubt in his mind but that this time it would be a boy. As it happened, the third child likewise was a girl. These were days of large families," Mrs. Ufford reminded me, "and may I say that the fourth child was a girl, the fifth child was a girl, the sixth child was a girl, and the time came when the seventh child was on the way.

"The Hartwells then were living in South Carolina. Luther Rice, our pioneer missionary, had just opened the gate to the Hartwell home one day and was walking up the front walk, when the nurse called down from upstairs to my Grandfather Hartwell: 'You have a baby boy. Your son has arrived.' Grandfather rushed down the front walk and threw his arms around Luther Rice for sheer joy. As the boy grew up, his parents said nothing to him about their hope that he would become a missionary. If he were to go as a foreign missionary, they wanted him to go, not at their behest, but to be a God-called man.

"After graduating from Brown University, he said to his parents, 'I have news which may shock you. I have decided to give myself to the mission field and to go to China.' The delighted parents then revealed to him that this decision was the answer to their prayer."

This young Hartwell went to China, where he served many years as a missionary. He had four children. All four of the Hartwell children became missionaries. These four children had children who in turn became missionaries. (One of these was Mrs. Ufford, of East China.) This means that of this one family came twelve missionaries who gave a total of three hundred years of missionary service to China. What an amazing result from Grandfather Hartwell's pioneer missionary devotion!

Their Spirit of Democracy

BAPTISTS HAVE FLOURISHED in spite of their devotion to independence and democracy — this astonishes men of churches having strong central authority.

When Dr. George Hooper Ferris was pastor of the First Baptist Church of Philadelphia (1905-1917), he sat one day beside a priest of the Roman Catholic Church.

The priest asked, "Dr. Ferris, where is your headquarters control or central authority which regulates your denomination?"

"We have no central authority which controls our denomination," replied the Baptist pastor.

The priest threw up his hands, amazed if not horrified at a church having no supreme authority.

"What!" he exclaimed. "No group of men or supreme bishop with authority to rule over your churches?"

"Absolutely none," answered Dr. Ferris.

Unable to conceive of a church with no earthly dominating authority, the priest said, "Well, my friend, all I can say to this is, 'May God help you.'"

Dr. Ferris replied, "That is exactly what he does!"

Their Meeting Houses, Baptisms, and Discipline

BAPTISTS WERE PIONEERS — and poor! On seeing the now prosperous Baptist Church of Clarks Grove, Minn., one finds it difficult to realize the hardships endured by the founders of it. We read that "a godly woman, in order to save her only pair of shoes, would walk barefooted, with her stockings and shoes in her hand, until about at the church," when she "would put them on and proceed."

169

In the early days, many of the poor but devout members came to this church in wooden shoes. Two men, who were living in a log house, did not have suitable clothes to attend church, "so one bought some overall material, and the other paid for having it made up, and then they took turns going to church on alternate Sundays."

Church edifices usually were plain buildings, little better than barns. Some were log cabins. Often they had no heat or had only primitive forms of heating. The King's Creek Baptist Church in Ohio, in 1816, built a log house twenty-six by twenty feet. Since the building had no fireplace and no chimney, heat was provided by a "box of wooden planks, twelve by six feet, partly filled with clay pounded in to form a bowl to hold the glowing charcoal, which afforded the only warmth for the bitter cold days." Writes the historian of the church, "That the carbonic acid gas did not send them all over Jordan is sufficient evidence that there was no lack of ventilation. The faithful sat on rough planks and sang, 'O God, the spring of all our joys.'"

These early Baptists held to believer's baptism. In Jefferson, Ohio, in 1833, a deacon who had recently arrived from Scotland carried the water one-eighth of a mile to fill the baptistry for the first baptism — "Trudging through the snow, he almost wished he was a Pedobaptist, but comforted himself with the thought that the candidate was small and wouldn't require much water." This sounds like Scotch comfort!

In Globe, Ariz., a non-Baptist demanded: "Why do you Baptists want a church here? You can't get any water around here." To which one of the ladies replied, "Sir, you could put our bunch of Baptists on the desert of Sahara — and we'd find water!" Actually, there was not enough water to make a pool in Pinal Creek. "The Ladies' Aid went to work and made a baptistry of heavy ducking, and with the aid of the men of the church, it was hung from posts on Central Hill, and filled by buckets of water, and we baptized four candidates, not on a desert, but on a very dry hill."

The current appraisal committee used in our denominational sector projects today is shown to be an idea borrowed from the Millbury Baptist Church in Massachusetts in the early days. It is recorded, in the history of that church, that "a board of assessors decided what each member should pay, and failure to pay was cause for discipline." Another church appointed assessors to appraise each man's property and assess him what he ought to pay, even beyond his voluntary subscription.

Pastors usually had very small salaries, as too often they do now. At Millbury in 1841, Pastor Fitts, "unable to support his family comfortably, and embarrassed in the business world, made known his intention of resigning as pastor. The wolf entered his door, and he left them April 1, 1843." The same wolf has been prowling around Baptist parsonages ever since!

This same church was challenged in vain by the Rev. Cyrus Tucker in 1853. He made it known, "that unless the people arise, and build a meetinghouse at once," he would resign. It is recorded, "We let the brother go with best wishes for his future success."

These early Baptists were sturdy and full of stamina, determined in their adherence to the principles of a free church and a free democracy. In the New England states, the Congregational Church was the established church and was supported by taxes levied and collected by town officials. In Blue Hill, Maine, for instance, the Baptist pastor refused to pay his tax for the support of "Father Fisher," the redoubtable pastor of the Congregational church. Forthwith, the town officials seized the good Baptist pastor's cow. But a Baptist layman was not such an easy mark, for he drove off the town officials with his scythe, and never paid the tax.

In a Massachusetts town, one Baptist layman threatened the tax collector, Sprout by name, in a note dated October 14, 1771: "Mr. Sprout, as a friend to you, I would warn you to forbear to proceed any further in that cursed thing as to pretend to carry men to jail for minister's rates; for if you do carry Andrew Perkins to jail, as the Lord liveth thou shalt surely die, and very likely in a sudden manner; therefore, see that thou art prepared to die, for before you arrive at Plymouth you may be in the eternal world." Here was 171 "zeal without knowledge" — a characteristic that still plagues some Baptists.

In Suffield, Conn., the attempt to build a Baptist meetinghouse on Town Street near the established church evoked a strong spirit of opposition. On the eve of the "raising" of the meetinghouse, the timbers were mutilated, and parts of the frame were hidden in wells. This first meetinghouse, opened in the years 1808-1810, was very plain. It was called "The Old Barn." It had rude slab benches, with a few chairs for aged women. Not until 1819 were pews put in and a pulpit placed against the wall. One finds it hard to realize this when one sees the beautiful, white, colonial New England church now in Suffield, across the greensward, and opposite Suffield Academy, a Baptist preparatory school.

It should be remembered that the early Baptist church edifice was called "The Meeting House." The first meetinghouse for Baptists in Greenbrier, W. Va., was built of logs, twenty-five by seventeen feet, a "chimney in the middle, in the breadth of the house." When next this church built a meetinghouse, it was a frame structure, forty by fifty feet. "A gallery ran around three sides of the room for the use of the slaves. The pulpit was high enough for the minister to see both floors. No intermingling of the sexes was permitted. When a man brought his wife or best girl to church, she sat on the south side with the sisters. The man sat with the brethren, if he was a brother; if not, he sat in the east corner with the sinners and bad boys." Since there were few clocks or watches in those days, the minister announced the time of the evening service by saying, "There will be services at early candle-lighting." There were wooden brackets hung up around the meetinghouse on nails, and tallow dips, brought to the church by people living nearby, were stuck in each bracket.

In Glasgow, Mont., the church began in a tent. "When the weather became too cold, services were held in the Odd Fellows' Hall."

When one thinks of the staid state of Vermont with its fine New England culture and traditions, one is surprised to find that Vermont was once a frontier territory, and that in 1786 there were no more than two or three thousand people in all the state of Vermont. The Massachusetts Baptists sent Jonathan Going out to this frontier territory to preach the gospel "to the Indians and *the other heathen in Vermont.*"

These Baptists believed in church discipline. In Holden, Mass., in 1809, one of the sisters transgressed as follows: "Sister C———— went over to Hubbardston and worshipped in what they call a church, with unbaptized persons!" Also in 1809, Sister P———— was brought up for discipline and "after considerable conversation on both sides, the church imputed some part of her misconduct to ignorance . . . she being a woman." In 1810, the church "labored with Brother C———— on account of his refusing military duty."

Reading the histories of the early Baptist churches, certain facts stand out in bold relief. American Baptists had rugged convictions. They held firmly to their principles. They maintained strict discipline. They were original, stubborn, and resourceful. They sacrificed to build churches on new frontiers. Despite their limitations and human frailties, they were worthy of all admiration. Nothing would do us all more good than a dose of this early Baptist elixir.

As this new space-age dawns, the distinctive Baptist principles of biblical integrity and spiritual freedom are proving unchanging resources of strength. Time has brought vindication also to the Baptist witness to believer's baptism. It is being ever more widely accepted. Since their humble beginnings in England and America, Baptists have grown steadily in number. Today, Baptists are found in seventy of the nations of the world, and they have a membership of more than twenty million.

BIBLIOGRAPHY

Backus, Isaac, *Church History of New England*. Philadelphia: American Baptist Publication Society, 1844.

Bicknell, Thomas W., *The Story of Dr. John Clarke*. Providence, R. I.: Published by the Author, 1915.

Brittain, Vera, *Valiant Pilgrim, The Story of John Bunyan and Puritan England*. New York: The Macmillan Co., 1950.

Burr, Agnes Rush, *Russell H. Conwell and His Work*. Philadelphia: The John C. Winston Co., 1917.

Burrage, Henry S., *Baptist Hymn Writers and Their Hymns*. Portland, Me.: Brown, Thurston & Co., 1888.

Carey, S. Pearce, *William Carey*. London: The Carey Press, 1934.

Clement, A. S., *Baptists Who Made History*. London: Carey Kingsgate Press, 1955.

Cooke, John Hunt, *Johann Gerhard Oncken: His Life and Work*. London: S. W. Partridge and Co., 1908.

deBlois, Austen Kennedy, *Fighters for Freedom*. Philadelphia: The Judson Press, 1929.

Deen, Edith, *Great Women of the Christian Faith*. New York: Harper and Bros., 1959.

Hines, Herbert Largo, *Clough: Kingdom Builder in South India*. Philadelphia: The Judson Press, 1929.

James, Powhatan W., *George W. Truett*. New York: The Macmillan Co., 1939.

Landis, Benson Y., *A Rauschenbusch Reader*. New York: Harper and Bros., 1957.

Little, Lewis Peyton, *Imprisoned Preachers and Religious Liberty in Virginia*. Lynchburg, Va.: J. P. Bell Co., Inc., 1938.

Mays, Benjamin E., *A Gospel for the Social Awakening: Writings of Walter Rauschenbusch*. New York: The Association Press, 1950.

Morrison, J. H., *William Carey, Cobbler and Pioneer*. London: Hodder and Stoughton, 1920.

Nelson, Wilbur, *The Hero of Aquidneck*. Westwood, N. J.: Fleming H. Revell Co., 1938.

Nelson, William Hamilton, *Tinker and Thinker, John Bunyan, 1628-1688*. Chicago, New York: Willett, Clark and Colby, 1928.

Payne, Ernest A., *The Great Succession*. London: Carey Press, 1946.

Pollard, Edward B. and Gurden, Stephen Daniel, *Luther Rice: Pioneer in Missions and Education*. Philadelphia: The Judson Press, 1928.

Robertson, Archibald Thomas, *Life and Letters of John Albert Broadus*. Philadelphia: American Baptist Publication Society, 1901.

Ryland, Garnett, *The Baptists of Virginia*. Richmond, Va.: The Virginia Baptist Board of Missions and Education, 1955.

Sharpe, Dores Robinson, *Walter Rauschenbusch*. New York: The Macmillan Co., 1942.

Thomson, Ronald W., *Heroes of the Baptist Church*. London: The Carey Kingsgate Press, 1937.

Torbet, Robert G., *The Baptist Ministry: Then and Now*. Philadelphia: The Judson Press, 1953.

Underwood, A. C., *A History of the English Baptists*. London: The Kingsgate Press, 1947.

Wolf, Wm. J., *The Almost Chosen People: A Study of the Religion of Abraham Lincoln*. New York: Doubleday and Co., Inc., 1959.